Reflections:
An Oral History of Detroit

Reflections:
An Oral History of Detroit

Irene Rosemond
Interviewer

Broadside Press
Detroit, Michigan
1992

Broadside Press
P.O. Box 04257
Detroit, Michigan 48204

ISBN: 0-940713-08-X
LCN: 92-90956

This book is dedicated to those who cared enough
to share their stories

ACKNOWLEDGMENTS

Special thanks to Irene Rosemond, interviewer; Katherine
Uicker, chief librarian at Elmwood Branch and assistant
librarian, Eileen Sullivan; City of Detroit Neighborhood
Opportunity Fund, George Lee for cover design and
Joann M. Cox, typesetter.

COVER PHOTOGRAPHS:

Barthwell's Drug Stores, courtesy Sidney Barthwell, Sr. and
Atty. Sidney Barthwell, Jr.; Atty. and Mrs. Willis M. Graves,
courtesy Irene Graves: Greenfield's Shoe Hospital, courtesy
Mary E. Cleveland; 1939 Chrysler Factory, courtesy
National Automotive History Collection, Detroit Public
Library.

Contents

INTRODUCTION

Promised land or landscape of industrial ruin? What, exactly, is the goodness of this city? What is its horror?

To answer these questions, one must know what Detroit has been. Only those who have experienced it can accurately access the rugged elegance of a place that once afforded the "good life" to millions of people.

The following accounts are the result of numerous taped conversations. There were technical problems, to be sure, but we trust that the participants will forgive any inaccuracies and accept our gratitude for their patience in completing this project.

In their own words
In their own way
Reflections...

Hilda Vest
Editor
June, 1992

JIM RAMSEY REMEMBERS DOWNTOWN DETROIT

I am going to focus on a lot of things that happened in the past and bring them to the present. We travelled a long ways and it is interesting that we can recall certain things. In my case it is like walking backwards and starting all over again. Where we live now is on Chene and Lafayette and that is where I started years ago. When I say years ago, I am referring to me at the age of seven or eight and I am eighty three years old now. Chene and Lafayette has a Farmer Jack now but during my time it was a candy store where I used to pick-up my newspapers for delivery. Now, if you're of the present, you don't see what I see. I mean I see the place where I go to pick up my papers, come back up Chene, go over to Macomb, past Orleans, Rivard and Russell. I'd go all through there, make a turn and come back. There was a lot of houses and stores there but it is not that way now.

Seventy years ago, when I was a kid, my aunt lived in a house directly on the corner of Chesnut and Orleans. There was a railroad that came through there, and Pittman Dean Ice Company and a coal station. There was a community center near my aunt's house where kids could congregate. We would go there and have a lot of fun on Friday nights. On Catherine Street, where the street cars went by, was Turner's Hall. We used to have dances there. During those days, it wasn't a matter of getting into trouble; it was a matter of having a good time, eating hot dogs, and drinking pop. When it was all over, we'd go home. We all went home on foot, not in cars. We'd walk our girls home and then went together in groups to whatever section we lived in. Walking back home was a lot of fun.

Now I am focusing on the area of Chene and Gratiot where I go and get my morning Free Press, then work my way downtown. I come down Hastings and Gratiot to right there where Adams comes through. This is where the street cars turn to go north. I do down to St. Antoine where there is a famous drugstore where everybody stopped to get their patent medicines. In the next block is the Cohen Theatre where friends meet. Then, I know you've heard of the Rose Bud Theatre. Further down from Broadway is a great big building, a beautiful furniture store.

I used to sell the Free Press at night at the corner of Broadway and Gratiot. There used to be a wagon that would come in around six or eight o'clock at night and stay there all night selling coffee and doughnuts. There used to be a theatre where Crowley's was built and the Broadway Strand. These places have been gone a long time. On the corner was Sam's. I used to sell the original Sam his paper. Next to Sam's was a penny arcade and a theatre where we used to go to see Tom Mix. There was a Burlesque house, farther down Farmer was another penny arcade and another Burlesque show. There was another theatre, I think it was the Mayfair Theatre, just at the point of hitting Woodward. There was also the Monroe Theatre where on the side was a water trough for the horses. Across the street was the Majestic Building, which was a famous building in its time. I'm sorry they tore the old City Hall down. There was Kern's on the corner which didn't particularly cater to Blacks. When they had to, they went out of business. Now, on the Kern block, behind Hudson's near the library is where the Kern clock used to be. People would say, "Meet me under the clock."

Coming up Woodward was Sander's Bakery, B. Siegel, the five and ten cent store, the original Woolworth's. I was going to Cass Tech and working across the street when they dug the foundation at the John Henry Men's Clothing store for the Cadillac Hotel on Washington Boulevard. Washington Boulevard was a very exclusive street. I remember this cafeteria owned by Jews where people would line up but they didn't want Blacks in there. There was the Hotel Statler, Ciro's, a

14

synagogue where the gas company is now, and an old fashioned hotel where the bus depot is now. On both sides of Woodward were stores, restaurants and Burlesque houses leading down to the river. This was on a slant in those days and the street was all brick. Where Ford Auditorium is now it was nothing but stores, movies houses and places where people would congregate on the street. The Union Railroad Station was down there, which hardly anyone remembers now. There were lots of warehouses, wine houses and places to drink. That is where we had most of our problems.

They ruined those nice houses. The Jews had maids to clean those huge apartments and what not. The whites then moved to Grosse Pointe. We were the reapers of what was left. We got the left-overs, after things were used up. When we got in there, it was no good. We had to do all kinds of repairs on the houses, the pipes were corroded. It's a disgrace that when we get it, it's ruined and we can't get ahead because of having to do repairs all the time.

I realized that I had to be exceptional because I graduated from high school at the age of fifteen. I had a mechanical background and as a mathematician and the teachers were really impressed with my performance. My folks didn't understand my capabilities or potential and neither did I. It wasn't their fault, they didn't know. A lot of people talk about how their parents didn't help them, but their parent's couldn't because they didn't know due to their non-exposure. They couldn't help themselves. During that particular time, people who made five dollars a day were really something. My father did not make five dollars a week. I was always a little ahead. I worked on Model T cars in the alley when I was eight or nine years old.

I remember a policeman named Foots, a Black man who kept everyone and everything in line. He didn't use a gun, but would hit people on the head with his stick. He was a big fellow. He would walk up and down Hastings Street. In those days, you could lay drunks on their front door and not have to worry.

When I was a little boy, I was very enterprising. My two neighbors, on either side of me, were German and Polish and when they couldn't find their children, I went to the store for them. My father was like that. He used his brain and was very comfortable in his later life. That was the way I saw it. If you didn't want to do something, don't. I'll do it but you have to pay me. You could borrow money, if you were able to pay it back, and we would both benefit. If payday was a few days away, people could come to see me, a kid of ten years of age, and borrow fifty cents or a dollar, which was a small fortune then. I'd ask them how much they would pay me when they got paid? They'd say, "You got it? I'd say, Didn't say that, but I can get it. But you must pay me!"

I ended up in Newark, New Jersey. I visited a lot of places out there. That is where I met my wife. I met her one day when I was on my way to church. We were introduced and when I came back from church, she was waiting for me. I went by her house, later. We met a few more times, went to a few places together and after we'd been acquainted for a while we went to New York, accompanied by a friend of hers, and got married. In Irvington, New Jersey is where I started a business, but I sold it because I wanted to come home.

We've raised six kids and put them all through school. Some of the top people in the State Department are my children. All of the labor analysts in the State of Michigan are under the jurisdiction of my daughter. My youngest daughter is forty years old and looks like she is sixteen. She had a four year scholarship to the University of Detroit through Head Start. She was the only child I had help with. The rest I had to do myself. At the graduation, ninety out of one hundred and six students graduated with honors. We sat there and heard them read out the names of all those who were given honors, but they wouldn't publicly announce the blacks who received honors. Their names were printed on the program. That's how prejudiced they were then. They wouldn't openly give Blacks any recognition. My philosophy is that I'm not going to sell myself short because of someone else's prejudice. I am going to let the white man know that I'm as smart as he is, in a nice way. And he's going to get out of my way. You don't have to raise your voice to let someone know you don't like the way they treat you. Do it humbly and intelligently.

MARY E. GREENFIELD REMEMBERS BREITMEYER SCHOOL, THE SCHOOL OF COMMERCE AND THE NORTH END

My mother, Mary Ezel Welch Greenfield, and my
father, Eugene John Greenfield, came to Detroit in 1920. I
was three years old at the time. We first lived in a home on
Katherine, between Dubois and Chene Street. We lived
there six months until my father found a home on what was
called the North End. We moved to 1529 E. Euclid between
Riopelle and the railroad.

My father was a businessman and had a small shoe
repair called Greenfield Shoe Hospital. The first location of
the shoe shop was at East Euclid near the corner of Cameron
Street. At that time, Sherrard Jr. High School had not been
built. There were houses along that side of the street. I
started school at Breitmeyer Elementary. Over the next few
years the houses on the south side of Euclid were torn down
to make way for Sherrard. I finished at Breitmeyer and
proceeded to Moore for the seventh and eighth grades
because there wasn't enough room at Sherrard. Breitmeyer
Elementary School was located on Cameron and Marston. It
was closed last year. At Moore, part of the school was
sectioned out for what they called "bad boys." I didn't like
going there but I really had no problems. I graduated from
Sherrard Jr. High in 1929. I was two years ahead because I
had gone to summer school three times. At elementary
school I didn't know a lot about racism at the time, but I
recall that when we played circle games in the gym, if I
happened to be standing next to a white student, that
student would drop my hand and move some place else.
This happened a few times. I also remember I wanted to be
in a play and raised my hand many times. I didn't realize
until later that I wasn't chosen because of racism.

In the ninth grade we were asked to decide if we
would take commercial courses, practical arts or college
preparatory. One had to be an A or B student, and I was.

18

All of the white kids took commercial cooking or college prep and all the Black kids, no matter how smart they were, took shop for boys and home economics for girls. I decided I would take commercial courses. My homeroom teacher, Ms. Hudson, took me aside and asked me why was I taking commercial courses? She said, "Your kind of people will never get a job in an office. I was never sassy in school, but I did say to her, "I think my mother can teach me all the cooking and sewing I need to know. I want to learn something in school that my mother can't teach me. Besides, when I get older I probably won't need to work." Of course that turned out to be the joke of the century. I think so many times on how much I depended on that commercial course. I followed through with it at the School of Commerce, which was located across the street from Cass Technical. Just like at Cass, one had to maintain an A or a B average to remain at Commerce. When I went to Commerce, there were very few blacks and only about six Black boys at that time. I graduated from Commerce in 1933. My whole livelihood was based on my commercial training. I had some college but didn't finish.

I remember when we went to Belle Isle there was a park on the Jefferson side called Electric Park. I used to love going there. They had one roller coaster ride where the cars ended up in a little bit of water. One of the highlights of going to Belle Isle was going to Electric Park. It later moved to Eight Mile and Gratiot and was known as Eastwood Amusement Park. The other thing I remember, especially about Belle Isle was that there was a ferry that would take you from Jefferson across to the island for five cents. I always enjoyed that ride very much. They had a bigger zoo than they have now. I enjoyed walking around watching the animals.

We moved to 8620 Greeley into an attic of a family and stayed there for a few months until the house across the street, 8621 Greeley, became empty. By that time my

19

father's shoe shop was on Russell, the fourth door from the corner of Alger, going north. It was across the street from the Russell Street Baptist Church. The church was a frame structure and faced Alger. Now, they've built a new church and the entrance is on Russell Street. Next door was E.M. Mason Funeral Home that later moved to Oakland and Alger. It is still there and is run by his children.

We moved from Greeley and lived for about two years or so at 987 E. Philadelphia between Cameron and Oakland. In May of 1919 we moved to where I'm living now; 637 Mt. Vernon, west of Oakland Avenue. At the time the Depression hit, the city went broke and everything was in bad shape. My father went out of business and stored his machinery in our garage. We had a couple rooming in the house with us. The man worked for the city garbage department and paid rent to us in script. That was all I had to pay my dues for graduation and I recall they had a conference to discuss whether or not they would accept script. This is how the teachers were paid. Everybody who worked for the city was paid in script which was later redeemed.

I graduated two years early so I was fifteen years old. We graduated in May instead of June because of the shortage of money. I worked part time typing for various people in the neighborhood, then got a job working for a spiritualist, Reverend Colbert. Then I worked for Hasker Gary Real Estate. He had an office on Russell between Wellington and Philadelphia. Our neighborhood, this entire area, was pretty well mixed. It was mostly white people, Italian and Polish. Some evenings they would sit on their porches playing the accordion. Further back, when I was younger and living on East Euclid, I remember a Polish wedding. The festivities lasted all day. I remember the accordions and people coming and going.

Of course we had street cars and the fare was six

cents and a penny for a transfer. At the foot of Woodward was the dock for the Bob-Lo and the old Vernors Ginger Ale plant. On the way to and from Bob-Lo you could stop and get a Vernors. There were more than just the Bob-Lo boats, there were Tasmo and Put-In-Bay, also. Usually Black people would have the boat on Monday. Many of the churches would rent the boat as a fund raiser, so many of the Black people only went on the days it was rented to Blacks. The same was true of the Graystone Ballroom. Blacks were able to rent the ballroom on Monday. I remember going there. We wore formals and the boys bought us corsages. We heard such band leaders as Duke Ellington, Cab Calloway, Count Bassie and Lionel Hampton. You name it, all the big bands came there. We danced on Monday nights in all of our finery and it was a special treat in the summer when we were able to dance outside in the garden. We thought that was very romantic. Believe it or not, afterwards we got on the street car, girls in their formals and boys all dressed up. This was our mode of transportation.

My family had a car when I was about six years old. It was a Chevrolet touring car and the top would let down. Sometimes when we would go some place on Sunday, I was allowed to bring one or two friends along. There was room for a couple of small chairs in the back. We would drive to Mt. Clemens where my father knew people, or we would drive as far as Port Huron. We had street cars called the inter urban which were sort of like trains that ran out Gratiot to Mt. Clemens, maybe to Port Huron. We had such a car on Woodward and we could ride out to Palmer Park where the street car turned around. Farther into the park there was this old log cabin. I think it was built by Pingree, but I'm not positive on that score. Anyway, we could go through the house. It was furnished and kept as sort of an historical monument. I understand this was like a summer home for them with a lake in front of it. Later on it was given to the city.

21

Oakland Avenue was a very busy street. There were a lot of small businesses, stores, cleaners and my father's shoe repair shop. Farther down Oakland, farther north, there was another Black shoe maker, beauty shops and pool rooms and banks. It was really lively. And then if you went as far north as Westminister, people called that Jew Town. Those stores would be open on Sunday in the early 30's and 40's. The merchants would put their merchandise out on the street. We would go down there to the fish and poultry markets. In the chicken market they would kill it and cut the head off and clean the feathers off the chickens there. We'd buy fish but they weren't cleaned too good and when we'd get home we'd have to scale them again. Scales would go all over every place. I hated that. My father used to like the necks and the feet which meant we had to clean the skin off the chickens. During the Depression, somebody got the bright idea, somebody down near Cameron, off of Holbrook, to clean the chickens and cut them up. Everybody would go there, even if it was out of the way. We would go there to get chickens, cleaned and cut up.

The Fisher Theatre was a movie house and it was in walking distance from our house. It was done in Aztec architecture. We really felt we were going someplace when we went to the Fisher, usually on the weekends. In that area, which is now called the New Center Area, near Woodward and West Grand Boulevard, for a couple of blocks either way it was real good shopping. Sometimes at night my mother and I would go up there window shopping. The stores were brightly lit and people would walk up and down Woodward window shopping after going to the theatre downtown.

I guess the first urban renewal I was aware of was when they tore down houses and built the Brewster Projects. This was in the very late 30's and early 40's. That's when a lot of Black people began to move out to this area which they called the North End. It was a prized area. All of the professional people were moving out here. I always thought it was funny when I went to Mt. Olive Baptist Church on Willis and Brush and my friends there said I lived out in the country. After they started tearing down all those houses and people started moving out into our neighborhood, it was considered a very choice neighborhood.

When my mother joined Mt. Olive Baptist Church, it was located near St. Antoine and Mt. Elliot. Later, it moved to Willis and Brush to a place that had been a Jewish Synagogue. A few years later, after having financial troubles, the congregation lost that church and it was taken over by Ebernezer Methodist Church. They had it until it was torn down to make way for the medical center. That was also the church where Joe Louis had trained. There was a gym in the church and a lot of aspiring boxers used it.

Bethel A.M.E. was located on St. Antoine and Frederick. Across the street was Children's Hospital. My uncle, Alfred Greenfield, had a moving and storage office on St. Antoine and Farnsworth. Later he moved to St. Antoine and Warren, on the north side of the street where Bethel is now located. A few years later, he moved across the street on the south side of Warren where Plymouth Congregational Church is now located. My uncle later moved out to the Puritan and 12th Street area. He was one of maybe two other Black movers and had these large vans. For awhile he did inter-state moving until they passed a law prohibiting smaller companies from using the road. This naturally affected the Blacks and my uncle was limited to moving within the city limits and state limits. I don't know the politics of it.

Irene Graves Recalls Teaching Experiences and Her Husband, Attorney Willis M. Graves

I was a teacher and I liked community work. It is interesting. When I lived on the westside people cared about their community, kept up their lawns, and there was no gambling on the street. We had the best time organizing blocks. I had the help of a young gentleman who is a lawyer now, named Bill Price. Not that I'm different from anybody else, but when you do things like that, they make you president of the Westside Human Relations Council. The Council was started by Mr. and Mrs. Golder Smith and it met at the library on the Boulevard. We joined the "Help Keep Detroit Beautiful" campaign. Then my husband worked with the Westside Improvement Association Credit Union and when people would organize a block, I would get them to buy a share. We had a credit union building and offered a little reward for joining. Roger Senior, Mr. Morgan, Mr. Howell, Mr. Sylvester and Mr. Baker, along with my husband, started the credit union. They are all dead now. There is no credit union now, but the Nacirema Club is still there.

It was the place to go for forums and speakers. We used to have hundreds of people come in to hear the speakers. It was a wholesome environment. They'd pay fifty cents and they were members. They'd play the juke box, sometimes have hot dogs. But now that area looks like it's been a war there. When I first lived on Roosevelt and then my husband and I brought a place on Vinewood, there were men in the community who were interested in helping. Men like Roy Morrison and Ada Summers' husband, Dr. Whitby and his brother, Dr. Ira. They would fit right in, furnish refreshments and sometimes if some kid didn't have fifty cents, they would say "there's the money," and let them in. Back then there were businesses all up and down Milford street. I don't know why they disappeared.

I taught school for forty two years from 1924 to 1966. I started teaching at age eighteen and stopped when my husband became ill and wouldn't let anyone care for him but me. I thought, well you're only supposed to teach 30 years, but I could have taught till I was seventy one. I taught at Capron, Garfield and McGraw. Roosevelt was quite a prestigious school. We had fifteen hundred students and sixty teachers. I was a directing teacher for the College of Education and most people don't know that they would bring classes from Wayne State University and my children would give demonstrations of what could be done in groups.

All my children have become so important. I taught all subjects; social studies, auditorium, language arts and French. In elementary school, starting from the second grade to the eighth, I got to know my students so well. My mother would let me bring five of them home for dinner every Friday. They liked that and she would teach them proper etiquette. One of my students, Eloise Sullivan, called me from Chicago. She said, "Don't you remember when my mother died and you picked me up and carried me down the hall because I was crying? The principal, Ms. Green, said you must not hit the children and you explained you were taking me to the lunchroom because I had just lost my mother and was upset." Eloise had run across someone from Detroit and asked them if they knew me. They did and gave her my phone number. I remember Eloise as a cute little girl who lived with her grandmother. She still keeps in touch and sends me a Christmas card each year.

I never got to become principal. The first time I took the exam I passed and came out number one in the written part, but I fouled up on the oral exam. Dr. Rankin, Assistant Superintendent of Schools, was on the committee to give the oral. He said, "I would like to know why you are teaching children in the ghetto French when they don't even speak English well?" I

25

was really angry that he asked me that and I looked out the window at the Broadway Market. I was so mad. I said, "Dr. Rankin, I've been all over the world. Little Japanese dogs understand Japanese, Chinese dogs understand Chinese, French dogs understand French and if a dog can understand another language, so can God's human beings." He turned real red. I wasn't ready for that question so I didn't even look at him and told him exactly what I thought.

Later, my mother told me she hoped I never would get to be a principal because there wouldn't be anybody there but me and the children. I didn't get along well with adults and I didn't like following, fooling around and wasting time. She said my answer was very raw and what I should have said was, "They started teaching French to the elementary children when they had radio programs, so I had my husband buy a radio, we listened to it and thought it would be nice if my children could speak French." My mother said that would have been a high class answer, but my answer let him know I was one of those belligerent Negroes. I said I didn't see anything wrong with being belligerent if it's for a good reason. She said I didn't know how to go along with the flow. I felt they should not have taught me these things if they didn't want me to carry them out. I'll tell you my opinion. People are always saying the children can't learn. I say that's because you aren't teaching. All you have to do is teach.

Our mothers taught us mostly at home, and then at Sunday School they taught us. When I was small we had doctors, lawyers, teachers and ministers and we held them in very high regard. They were pace setters and were the heroes. I'm glad I came up in the era I did because I learned to recognize quality, value, culture and refinement.

I was educated at the University of Michigan before I went to Europe. They said in order to get a doctorate in language I would have to spend some time in France. I went to the University of Paris in 1938 because I had entered the doctoral program. I went to school there in August, did the summer session and started the September session. By October, Hitler was in Austria and war was breaking out. The French told the Americans to go home because they couldn't take care of anyone but their own. I stayed at the Sorbonne through September and had to come home in October. On my dresser I have a document from the director of the Sorbonne stating that Irene Graves has finished these many hours, but no graduation. I never would have gotten there in 1938 because we didn't have any money.

I received my Masters of Arts from McGill University and my room was right over the library. Every night I'd go to the library and stay up all night memorizing everything. When it came time to take the oral and written exams, I could speak just like the French book. That is how I won the Letter of Credit Award that paid for books, tuition, room and board at Apaneson d'Famique, one of the universities. I met Collins George one summer at McGill. He asked me how did I win that award? I said, "I studied." He was smart and he wouldn't have to stay up like I did. We were the only two colored people there. He went to all the night clubs and was a Phi Beta Kappa. Later he became publisher and editor for the Pittsburgh Courier, but the Detroit News took him away and he was a music critic. I went to visit him when he moved in this condominium. I took my friend, Jerry, down there to see it. I said, "Collins, you don't have the glass doors that go over the tub." He didn't know that he was supposed to have them and I said, "Come and look at the model." He said, "Here you are, taking over like at McGill." Afterwards, he wrote me a letter and said "thank you and there you were taking over." He's dead now.

There were not many Black teachers in Detroit when I taught elementary. Most of them were real light, not brown like I am. I was the blackest teacher there. Katy Fuller, Jerry Snead and Edith White all were light. They were good teachers. The principal, Mr. Randall, asked me if I would mind telling him if Ms. Watts is white or colored? I said, "I really don't know, I'm new at this school." I knew she was colored but she was blond with light eyes. She was from Atlanta and had a degree. I've always been like that when they start asking me things that I didn't want to answer. Another excellent teacher was Nellie Watts, who bought Marian Anderson and Paul Robeson here to Masonic Temple. I remember going to hear Duke Ellington in the same place where the symphony goes now.

When I was a little girl, my mother took me to hear Marian Anderson. I learned later, when I went to Europe, how they worshipped her there. I was in awe of her because she was just majestic and very regal and had a wonderful stage presence. I remember going to hear Booker T. Washington and I said to my mother, "I don't think he is such a good speaker. Who ever heard talk of if a man is in a ditch you pull him down in the ditch and it's no need for you to stay down there with him?" My mother said, "That's good for you to think about. It means levels, cast-system levels." I didn't think he was so hot. She also took me to hear Roscoe Conklin Simmons. He said, " on up ship of state, on up union strong and great. Humanity with all its fears and all its joys and all its tears will never decide my fate. I am the captain of my fate." I told mother I liked him. I liked the rhyming. He would hold you on the edge of your seat if you were a little girl or boy. But older people liked Booker T. Washington because he said, "Train the mind and the hand." I found out later he was right because my brothers could really do everything with their hands; paint and nail. I could do nothing with my hands. No cooking, no washing dishes. My mother was a good cook so I just didn't. It is a skill though and some of us just can't do it. I follow the recipe and it still isn't any good.

I did a history of the Negro calendar for Diggs Enterprises that covered 1941 to 1962. I still have some of them. I took pictures from Ebony magazine and enlarged them. Those people had jobs and were in what Ebony called the Hall of Fame. Diggs, Senior is the one who did the calendar, before his son was a congressman. It was time consuming and I had to do a lot of research. Oh, I enjoyed it! I went to the Schomburg Collection in New York, the University of Michigan, the morgue of the Times. We don't have the Times now. I went to the Free press and the News. They let me have information about things that happened among Detroiters. They told me about the lovely plaque downtown on Griswold Street, marking the place where the salves were harbored overnight. I took a picture of it and put it in one of the calendars. I got four hundred dollars at the time and it took care of my travel and materials.

I went to Africa and Diggs, Senior was so pleased because I talked to outstanding Africans. The Africans did not seem to like Negroes and still aren't all that fond of them. Sometimes they appeared to be envious. They felt if they had the opportunities we have, they could do so much for their people. I can understand the envy. We live in hotels and they lived in those little huts. In 1967, I received the Carter G. Woodson Award of Distinction for Negro History for doing those calendars. I don't think anybody else in Detroit ever received it.

In my living room there are a lot of things from my sorority that show they approved of what I did. I became Regional Director when I was very young. I had never been the president of any chapter and they had to get a new amendment that said you did not have to be a president of a chapter first. I would just go on and do just like my mother said, "There she goes, bookety book." I've always been like that. I also received the Baptist Sister Award. They enlarged a picture of me and gave it to me at an affair. It was for my helpfulness to my children who I took from my school and put in fashion shows. People like for you to do things with children. I think you can say I've paid my dues. The group called the Co-ettes once nominated me for a Golden Heart Award for my volunteer work. The children were all so lovely, long ago.

My grandfather was the governor of Tennessee. I used to ask my mother, "Who was that white man with the mustache?" She said, "Governor Patterson, your grandfather." I said, "My grandmother's name wasn't Patterson, it was Banks." My mother said, "She was his housekeeper. There are six in the family and all of them were sent to school by him." I said, "Mother take him out of my room. You've been telling me all along to have as many children as you wish, but be married." I was through with him, he had to go. She took him out of my room. I said, "He could have married her couldn't he?" She said no, because it would have been very revolutionary. My grandmother was beautiful, Indian and Negro. They loved their children. Remember Jefferson, how he sent all of his daughters to Europe because he wanted them well educated. He loved them and let everybody now they were his kids. I remember a conversation about it being better to help a large group of people because you can accomplish more than being involved with one. My grandfather perhaps did more as governor, rather than deciding he was just going to be with the one he loved. I regretted it that all my mother's family were little bastard children. They didn't even have his name. We got a lot of things from his house. My mother loved him, said he played pillow fights with them at night and rode them on his back. When the new ones came, he'd rock them to sleep. He was from Scotland. I guess he wasn't so prejudiced.

My husband, Willis M. Graves and I met at Dr. Sweet's house. Gladys Sweet and I went to teaching school together, but she didn't finish and married Dr. Sweet. Dr. Sweet and Graves went to Howard together. One day she said, "Come over, I want you to meet my

30

attorney." So I went to Christmas dinner and met him. She asked me how did I like him. I said, "He's too old for me." Dr. Sweet asked Graves how he liked me? He said, "She's not dry behind the ears yet." We didn't like each other at all. I had a birthday party and invited him. We were in there dancing and singing and he came to the door. He asked if Miss Graves was available and my mother said, "Yes I'll get her." But he said, "No, just give her this gift. It's from Mr. Graves." He gave me a beautiful brown silk umbrella. When my mother asked why didn't he come in, I said I guess he didn't like dancing and having a good time. He's old anyway. I told him once when we went to the Nacirema Club, "I've watched people this evening and although I'm the youngest thing here, I know as much as anyone around here." Graves said, "Well it's nice that you think that, but I think if you talked it over with your mother and father they would tell you different. You still have a long way to go to know as much as these people do." My mother was crazy about Graves. She said if she had anything to do with it I would marry him. She said I always think I know everything but I didn't. But I've always been like that, too. Maybe because I was the first born. My mother had to teach me not to be so outgoing. I asked her once why she put Albert at the head of the table when Daddy was not home? I'm oldest, but she said, "Because if God had meant for you to be first he would have made woman first. But he didn't. He made Adam first, so the head of this house is your father. But I want you to understand wherever you sit is the head of the table." I never could understand why Albert, ten months younger than me, would sit at the head of the table.

I should talk about my husband and all he did. When he joined the NAACP he told them, "Now this is not a political organization, this is a civil rights organization, so let's keep politics out of it." But they wouldn't do that because they wanted to be known as Democrats.

He said, "Now I'm going to be a Republican as long as I'm here and I'm going to do everything I can for civil rights. He was a good Republican. Everytime they ran a candidate, they'd ask Graves to speak. He called it the Grand Ole Party. I told him I didn't like it because you have to be rich. Graves said, "No you have to be dedicated. You have to appreciate that Abraham Lincoln gave you an opportunity to vote." I told Graves Lincoln didn't really mean to do it. He just didn't want the South to beat up the North. I'm not political and Graves said I never would be because I talk too much and tell everybody what I'm going to do. When you're political you don't tell people what you're going to do; you just do it. Sometimes you have to stop and think about the best procedure. Graves was the best. He never went out shouting at me. He would have been a good principal and come out number one in the oral exam because he would have answered so smoothly. He had a trained mind. He'd lose on one level, go to the Michigan Courts, lose and go to the Supreme Court and win. I'd have blown up before then and they would have put me in jail. Graves realized you couldn't do everything at one time.

Graves became the chairman of the Legal Committee here in Detroit. He had the help of other attorneys like Crockett, Dent and Roxborough. Graves and Dent received many awards. Dent was the one who did the Bob-Lo Case. He stopped it where if you were a Negro graduate you couldn't go to Bob-Lo. Graves had the Sipes Case where it allowed backs to live all over. I told him it was the worst thing that ever happened because everyone ran away after we moved here. But he said we were entitled to purchase wherever we were able to.

Lori Miller who lived on the west coast wrote a book that had a chapter about Graves in it. Then George Edwards, a federal judge, wrote a book that had a chapter on Graves and Dent. Graves made nice contacts. He was refined and gentle. People like you when you're quiet. They don't like you to muddy the waters. They were honored by the National Bar Association, the Omegas, and the Kappas. Graves received the Alumnus of the Year Award from Howard University. Mayor Cavanaugh declared Willis M. Graves Day and his picture was on the front page of the Free Press and the Detroit News.

My mother was a Republican until she died. I remember standing in the rain at election time and I told my mother, "I'm going to vote for Roosevelt." She asked why and I told her, "Because Hoover chased those people off the White House lawn and they were veterans." Mother said, "They had no business on the White house lawn." I said, "They had just as much right to be there as Hoover." Mother said, "Keep quiet now. You're lying. I don't want people to hear that you are not going to vote for our president." I voted for Roosevelt and my mother and dad voted for Hoover. When Roosevelt won they were so mad that nobody would say anything. I said, "Mother, our sofa is falling down, our lights have been cut off and I'm getting script." I said, "Let's try somebody else. You don't have to be mad. It's just one white man taking the place of another white man." They wouldn't say a word because I had talked about my voting for Roosevelt.

See, I always talked too much. I also voted for Mr. Lucas instead of Mr. Blanchard. I wanted him to be governor and didn't care that he was a Republican. I wrote a letter to the press saying that Lucas deserved to be governor. He stood in line with the Democrats for years and became the first black Executive of Wayne County. As soon as he became a Republican, they thought he should become governor. I said, "I think so, too," and wrote it to the press and signed my name. Father Dade asked me why did I write that letter. I said, "I wanted Lucas to get it." Father Dade said, "He's not going to get it." Lucas wasn't going to do anything against you. Let him get in there and do something wrong and he wouldn't have it very long. I'd jump on him along with everybody else. The NAACP made a statement and they came out

33

here because I am a member and they got so mad at me.
They said the majority voted against Lucas receiving a
civil rights position. I thought if anybody should have it,
Lucas would do better than a white man would. A white
man did get the position, but Lucas is still in that department getting $80,000 a year. Lucas wrote me a letter and
thanked me for being so brave. I thought to myself, "I
don't have anything to lose." What did I have to lose?

I saw Coleman Young on television when he was
just a youngster. I asked, "Who is that colored man?," and
Graves said, "He's got a good mind. He's going places." I
saw Mr. Lucas standing beside a white sheriff and
asked,"Who is that colored man?" Graves said, "That's
my fraternity brother and he's going places." And you
know what, neither one of them was doing any talking or
anything, but they had good ideas. They both went places.

FLOYD HENSON AND CHARLES BOOKER REMEMBER THE
NACIREMA CLUB

The Nacirema Club was founded in 1922 primarily
as a social club that would welcome the whole spectrum of
black people in Detroit. Other social clubs were for the
upper class, so this club was established on the premise that
any man of good moral character, regardless of his eco-
nomic and social status, was eligible. Blacks had nowhere
to socialize and the idea was to provide a place where
blacks could gather and enjoy some social activities. Edgar
Houston was the first president and John B. Abrams is
president now. The club has had twenty three presidents.

I remember when the club first opened, they had
dances here. The Nacirema Club was very well known.
We used to sponsor boat rides, sponsor baseball and
basketball games and have Easter Egg hunts for the children. We had a bowling league, spring dance and
Nacirema Week in August. In the late thirties and early
forties we had a membership of two hundred with a
waiting list just as long. Now our membership's less than
one hundred. Nacirema is a private club now and it's just
not as popular anymore. After the war and desegregation,
there were places you could go then that you couldn't go
before. Black people made an exodus to the suburbs, sort of
outgrew the neighborhood. We flocked to places that we
couldn't go to before.

Nacirema spells "American" backwards. Since we
were an American organization and supportive of American ideas, the name was unanimously accepted by the
founding members. Some people thought it was an Indian
name. We have quite a few awards from various organizations for involvement in social and civil rights works. We
support the NAACP and have a Life Membership and a
Gold Membership. We have also been involved with the
Boy Scouts. Throughout the years, we have had many

35

speakers, governors, mayors, legislators, business and professional leaders.

Dr. Wendell Cox of WCHB and WJZZ radio is one of our current members. He made arrangements for different members of Nacirema to give talks and recite poetry on black history during the month of February.

Some of our members are Councilman Clyde Cleveland, Attorney Horace Rogers, Urban League Director John Dancy, Probate Judge Willis Ward, Attorney Willis Graves, John Roxborough and other prominent people. Our members come from various church denominations. Each year we attend the church of a member and on Christmas day we have a high noon service for members and male relatives. A local pastor is invited to speak. Usually, we go to that church the following year or the previous year and make a donation. We have an annual Men's Day, an informal New Year's gathering, golf and bridge tournaments. The Nacirema Club plans to continue to publish a newsletter every month. It is called the Nacirema Highlights. We will have a Bowling League Banquet in April and a dinner dance is scheduled for June. Over the next five years we want to make some interior and exterior improvements, increase our membership, continue participating in CAUSE and being active in the Community Block Club.

The Nacirema Club is open to any organization that wants to have meetings here, so long as their group is sponsored by a member. We have three floors and a basement and we are still located at Milford and 30th Street.

SALLY JOHNSON REMEMBERS THE DEPRESSION

We didn't even recognize it as being a Depression because our mother always had an extra place at the table for someone. We enjoyed it. These are the things I thought were beautiful. So many of us don't want to talk about that and remember, but this was a situation we all went through, those of us that were there. I remember the Soup Kitchen. We had to eat in the Soup Kitchen. It was that or starve. It was fun to us, but it was a thorn in my mother's side. To think that her husband came all the way here and was not able to support his family. There weren't any jobs.

The kind of thing I want to focus on is the pride, care and love the families and neighbors had for each other. If someone moved into the neighborhood, people would bring food to the house. They would share, even though they didn't have any more than their neighbors.

We live in a materialistic society, today. Neighbors aren't what they used to be. Back then, what happened to one person was the concern of the whole block. This is no longer true. Now you are judged by what you own and what your status is.

Unidentified Speaker

I am a native Detroiter and I was born at the YWCA on Elizabeth, because it was a rare thing for blacks to go the hospital then. I was one of the last babies born there, a month before they moved everyone to the hospital, the new building in Highland Park. I lived in the "red light" district near Napoleon and Beaubien Street, which represented prostitutes, pimps and so forth. My father was always a caretaker, even though he worked at Ford Motor Company. A caretaker in those days took care of a building. Now they call them Building Managers. We were really very fortunate because he always had a job and we didn't have to worry about paying rent and things like that.

What I remember so much is we had hobos in those days and they would come to our back door. Mama would always fix them a plate and Daddy would let them sleep in the basement. Detroit is my city. If you can't make it in Detroit, you can't make it anywhere. It's just a wonderful place. I wouldn't live anywhere else. Once my husband and

I thought about moving to London, Ontario. but we soon gave that up. There's no place like Detroit.

GLADYS HUNTER REMEMBERS CHURCH EXPERIENCES

When I came to Detroit I was about 11 years old. I went to what was then the old Capron School on Riopelle near Russell. I graduated from there. Then we moved from Hamtramck and I went to Hamtramck High School. When we moved here we lived with my sister and her husband. They had smaller children and the landlords didn't like to rent to people with a lot of children. I remember moving into one place where my brother-in-law was going to hide us so they wouldn't think he had a lot of children. We were trying to find a permanent home but we moved several times trying to do this. When we moved back downtown, I attended Miller School.

I remember when I was living in the South I joined the Baptist Church when I was 10 years old. I was baptized a year before we came to Detroit. The Baptist Covenant says "as often as you move you must reunite to a church of your choice." So every time we moved I attended a new school and joined a new church.

Finally, in 1925, we moved into this area and seems that we've been here ever since. I joined Calvary Up On the Hill and we have been a member of that church for over fifty years. When I first joined, the girls sat on one side and the boys sat on one side. That was when I met my husband. He saw me, watched me grow from then on. When the other fellows started looking at me he would say, "That's mine." At that time we had not even spoken. So we got married and raised six children, five boys and one girl. My husband taught Sunday School and all my children were raised to attend Sunday School. One of my sons is an attorney. He is a supervisor in Probate Court. My oldest son lives in California. He's in Business Administration. My husband passed several years ago and it's been my responsibility to raise them and keep the family together. Everyone says, "You've done a beautiful job." I reply, "No, me and God." So, to me, Detroit has been my home ever since I came here. I have never thought of living any place else. My children and grandchildren are scattered across the United States. I have visited them, but have never had a desire to go and stay where they are.

Mrs. Hill Remembers Dr. Alvin Loving

When I was a student at Miller school, Dr. Alvin Loving was way before his time. He told the boys to keep their shirt tails in and the girls were told to keep their dresses down. We were encouraged to walk with pride and do our work. Dr. Loving would take us aside and talk to us. He would tell us, "Be proud of yourself." All these things went into shaping us. Our graduation class was really dedicated to him.

His brother was one of the first black counselors at Miller. He had patience and took time to go out to your home if things didn't seem right to him. Both Dr. Loving and his brother really loved the kids. Any problem you had, you could go to either of them.

We had a home economics teacher named Mrs. Pat Ellison. She was great with the girls. I found her about five years ago and told her "thank you." She taught us hygiene and so forth. I think that is what's lacking in our public schools today. Back then, you could feel the love in them. You could go to them and talk with them and they'd put their arm around you. They had time for you. I think that helps a lot. The teachers didn't make the money that is made today.

A friend of mine told me about her sister who had a lot of children. She would call my friend and ask her to help. After the fourth child she said, "I would just melt with each new baby." My friend worked for a very wealthy family as a live-in maid and did not have to use any of her monies to live. She was able to help her sister and brother-in-law often. Her sister ended up having nine children and my friend never knew what it was then to have her own money. The women who wanted children were blessed with children. The women who didn't would reach out and help. I asked my friend if that bothered her. She said, "No, that was my sister." She got annoyed with me for asking her that ques-

41

tion. Now she has grand nieces and great-grand nieces and I asked her, "Aren't you proud?" She said, "Well, I did wonder what it was to work and actually hold money in your hand." This is what I'd like to bring out, the continuity in the family. That is how strong the family relationships were.

REVEREND AND MRS. JOHN FORSYTH REMEMBER THE CHURCH AND MARRIED LIFE

I have been in the ministry for many years and did what you call counseling. I look back on that as being the best experience of my time. I can't say it was one hundred percent successful, but if just one person benefited, that was good. I've been doing weddings for 40 years. I never stopped to count how many. It would be interesting to read the records.

After retirement, John took a position at Orchard Lake Community Church. He counseled and married people who were non-members. Some of them sent him pictures. I was interviewing this photographer once and asked what made him interested in photography. He indicated that his interest stemmed from a desire to retain memories. They did this for him when he was growing up because they lived very modestly and couldn't afford to go many places. They relived things through the pictures. I was going to say that we have all these pictures and can't identify them. When I worked in the First Presbyterian Church, people would bring pictures and there would be nothing to identify who was in them or where they were taken.

When I came to Detroit in 1942, I met John Forsyth. I knew about him but didn't see him for 22 years. I married and so did he. My husband died, John became divorced, and after working for minsters for so many years, I married one. I continued to work after we married. He continued in his position. Wives don't come with the package. When I went to a church convention years ago, the other young wives of minsters let it be known that the churches had hired their husbands, but the wives didn't come with the package. They said they work and have their own responsibilities. I had no children, but John's children accepted me totally. They were old enough to take care of themselves. Suddenly, I had a family of four.

CLARE O'NEAL ADAMS RECALLS A FAMILY REUNION

We had a family reunion in 1986. That reminded me of my father's mother who I remember quite well, and also my mother's mother. My husband and I belong to the Genealogy Society and we were quite active in it at the time. I met a man who told me he had traced his family back to the 16th century. I asked him how many trips did he have to make to Scotland? He said he didn't have to leave the United States. All the history was tracked back from his mother.

FLORENCE WEEKS JONES REMEMBERS FAMILY LIFE

My Dad worked at the Panama Canal and was there
from 1905 to 1913. It's fascinating to hear him talk about the
things that happened there. He then went to Canada and
told me he went first class and was real proud. I remember
when I was fifteen years old my mother gave me a locket
that my father gave to me when I was five. My mother said,
"I kept it until I thought you had enough sense to keep it."
I've had it all these years. I stopped wearing it when the
lock broke. My father said he was on his way home from a
painting job on my birthday and he wanted to buy me
something. He saw this locket and purchased it for five
dollars in 1923.

I lost my brother, Barry, in 1989. His death almost
tore my family apart because he was the one member of the
family that we all loved. No matter how many brothers and
sisters you have, there's always going to be unintentional
preferences. He was very even tempered, had a gift for gab,
was a bachelor and everybody loved him. He lived in
California but he would always come home for Christmas.
Everyone just totally enjoyed him. When they called from
California, he was very sick and in Intensive Care. My sister
couldn't go and asked me. I said yes. When I got there he
was on a ventilator so I called my sister and told her if she
wanted to see Barry alive she better hurry and come. She
and another sister and brother came right away.

I have this book of nostalgia. I'm into genealogy.
My father's mother used to come down for visits, but I never
did think to ask her her mother's name. When I first started
talking to my father about the past, he was hesitant to talk.
He was about 80 years old and I didn't know how I was
going to get him to start talking. So, using a tape recorder I
would get him to say a few words. I would rewind the tape
and let him listen to it. After that he was okay. He said I
was a bastard child. If he hadn't told me that I would have

spent years trying to make links between the differences in names.

The other day my cousin told me, "I know all about your father's family." I said, "Oh my gosh, I've found a treasure." About two years ago I decided to collect as many family pictures as I could. Barry was an artist and I had things he drew and letters of commendation he received from professional associations. I also had my mother and father's marriage license. I kept these things for about a year before I could compile them without the hurt. About three months ago I finished. The locket from my father is in it. I have a friend who is really into genealogy and she sometimes asked why did I take all that time putting these things together when my family was not interested? I was thinking the other day, we all have reasons why we do certain things. We may not be able to understand it at the time, but there's some rationale behind it. My friend advised me to use a special kind of paper so that throughout the years it won't yellow and turn brittle. I put them on poster board and now I wish I'd used something more substantial. I have at the top my father and mother's names and the year that I did it, 1989. I had the pictures framed. If you don't put them under glass, they will fade and deteriorate. Even though it was painful, these were beautiful memories of happy times. I have tears every time I look at it.

Parents say they don't show partiality, but they do. My sister and I lived across the street from our father. When he was sick, I used to go over to his house every day and prepare his meals. The first thing he would ask is, "Have you seen your sister today? How is she doing?" I would say, "You know she could come over here at least once a day and say hello and see how you're doing." He'd jump to my sister's defense saying, "You know she works hard every day. She's tired." I worked too. However, he wouldn't even say hello to me. I'd go in and say, "Hi Dad, how are you?" He wouldn't say a word. But he did show his appreciation by sending me thank you cards all the time for coming over and taking care of him. My father used to love to send cards to people, all kinds of cards. He sent me thank- you cards and I kept them. One day, I thought, when he's gone, I'm going to put all these cards in a book. So I did. I put them in the keepsake album.

EARLE POOLE REMEMBERS ST. MATTHEW
A.M.E. CHURCH

I am a member of St. Matthew A.,M.E. Church
located at 9746 Petoskey Street in Detroit, between Chicago
and Boston Boulevard. When I moved to this area in 1947,
there was no church here. Not only were there no Negro
churches, the schools did not have any Parent Teacher
Associations. There was no need for PTA's at that time.
When we moved in problems began developing. The
neighborhood was lily white. We found ourselves in the
position of having to organize. The building of the express-
way through Black Bottom caused a lot of people to move
out this way. They didn't have any place to stay. Those
who had money purchased homes or rented a house and
soon it was over crowded.

When the 1960 census was conducted, I was appointed an area supervisor. I had thirty two people working
with me, counting people and trying to get the ones missed.
We were called a kind of clean-up squad for this area. On
Hazelwood, I found a mother and two daughters living with
a total of 24 people upstairs in a three bedroom apartment.
They were all on welfare. This is the kind of over crowding
that had developed before the riot and really was what
instigated the riot.

Reverend Hendre, a former Bishop and Presiding
Elder in Canada, returned to Michigan in 1953 and organized St. Matthew A.M.E. Church. Reverend Hendre had
been a member of Michigan annual conference and the only
way to re-enter was to organize a church. He was a very
educated man, knew how to do things and had the respect
of everyone. He walked this area and asked each family
from Webb to the Boulevard their name, address, telephone
number, and how many were in the family and what church
they belong to? When he had gotten all the information, he

picked out the A.M.E. Methodists and called us together at J.R. Smith's home. There were fifteen of us. He told us he was interested in having us organize a church. My first reaction was that I had just bought my home and did not have any money to build a church. But he was very persuasive. He encouraged us and showed us that nothing was impossible. That was the motivating spirit he had and he passed it on to each of us. He said, "Go out there and conquer the mountain," and you felt as if you could. We went to the Board of Education and got permission to hold services at Hutchins Jr. High School on Woodrow Wilson Street. We had our first service and first Sunday School there. We eventually moved to a spot on 12th Street. Rev. Abraham, who is still living, had organized the first church on 12th street. But we were here before Tried Stone Baptist Church.

Then he had Rev. Marvin McKendrick who said he wouldn't leave us. He organized our small church on 12th Street to get into the Conference, then asked the Bishop to give him a bigger and better church. The Bishop gave it to him and we were left carrying all the responsibility. We told the Bishop we wanted Rev. McKendrick back here because he had gotten us into this. We wanted him to be here to help us build, because we were renting then. Rev. McKendrick left us high and dry.

So Rev. Duncan came to us from Ebenezer A.M.E. Church. He was an assistant minister there and his mother had a lot of pull at Ebenezer. Rev. Duncan was just getting indoctrinated into the ministry, but under him we struggled and bought the church we are in now on Petoskey street.

We had quiet a few members that were not members of AME's. They moved into the area, but came to services out of friendship and became involved with us. The majority of blacks were accustomed to going to church and it may not have been the church of their denomination but it was in the vicinity and appealing because of the convenience. There was a Baptist family that joined St. Matthew because of that very reason. We also have a list of things from the Annual Conference that we are obligated to do in the community. We sponsor trips to Camp Baber, support education, the Easter Gleaners and support the missionary. We have no choice about getting involved in the community, as far as the A.M.E. Conference was concerned. We're assessed. At this time I was also a member of the West Grand Boulevard-Clairmount Improvement Association. We were active in that organization as well as in organizing the church.

My mother, Wesa Jones, was one of the first Deaconesses at St. Matthew. Other Deaconesses were Mrs. Brooks who lived on Blaine, Beaulah Smith, Mrs. Cobb, Mrs. Brim and Mrs. Cook. We also had Stewards, Mrs. Cruse and Mrs. Hewlett. You have to be a Steward before you become a Deaconess. Today, Rosa Parks, myself, Carrie Gaskin, Mrs. Harris, Mrs. Mitchell and Mrs. Brim are Deaconesses. The Stewards work close with the minister, visiting the sick, and doing what they can for the homeless. It's like a promotion, a place of honor to take care of those things. Stewards wear black caps and white dresses. A Deaconess is older, and is one that took the religious side more seriously, with more dedication. We're retired from the Steward side. We wore white uniforms or grey and black uniforms with a little black cap that has a white binding. We are not expected to participate in any of the services, but we have one day of recognition where we invite other Deaconesses. We teach the Stewards. We don't have Catechism, but Mrs. Booth teaches the Sunday School and is a beautiful teacher. She is almost like a minister, is very devoted as far as her secretary responsibilities are concerned and is always helping with the finances of the church. She also keeps the records for St. Matthew.

The reason Mrs. Rosa Parks chose St. Matthew is because her mother was a member here. She likes the friendliness that's shown there. Her mother and my mother were Deaconesses at the same time, in the early 1950's. Her mother is decreased now. It was not so much like home because her mother had attended St. Matthew, but she wanted a small church that was friendly. Our church is a family church where everybody knows everyone and is concerned about everyone. Now there are several generations. If a mother sang in the choir, the daughter and the daughter's daughter sang, too. It is really a family church and always has been. At graduation time every child that is graduating receives a gift and we have a special program for them. The church also sponsors the Missionary which gives baskets of food to the poor. We have three choirs.

Since its inception, in 1953, at the home of Mr. and Mrs. J.R.Smith at 1302 Hazelwood in Detroit, St. Matthew A.M.E. Church has had approximately thirteen different ministers.

RUTH TURBIN TRACES HER FAMILY HISTORY IN A
BOOK CALLED
TIPS OFF THE OLD BLOCK

My name is Ruth Turbin and I have written a
book, Tips Off The Old Block. In it I was able to trace
my history back five generations of the maternal lineage
and four generations paternal. On the maternal side, the
fist generation that we know about is my great-great
grand mother, Charity Cook Hunter, believed to be born
in Louisiana. Her master's name was Cook and she had
one daughter, Sarah Wilhelmina Cook. I tell you in the
book about how Master Cook had promised them their
freedom, had the will written up, but on his death the
lawyer destroyed the papers, then freed them. He took
the watch that had been given to Charity and sold them
into slavery in Mississippi to a planter named Hunter.
Sarah married Peter Price. He was born crossing the
ocean in 1841 and died in 1916. His trades were carpen-
try, shoemaking and farming. He worked in the field,
lived in Marx, Mississippi and his master's name was
Mr. Self. The Self's still own most of Mark, Mississippi.
Sarah had two daughters; my grandmother, Rosa Ann
Price, and Willie Charity Price. Rosa had six children,
three of them survived; my mother, James Price and
Henry Price. My grandmother also married Henry
Wilson Morgan and they had three children; Uncle Bud,
Vanessa, Morgan and Chester Morgan, They lived in
various places throughout the South. Rosa and Henry
Wilson Morgan were both teachers. My mother taught
school, also.

My mother met my father in the 1920's. My
father was centered in Kentucky. On my father's side,
the first person we remember being told about was
Sordela, my great grandmother. Her master's name was
Martin. She had four sons, Nathaniel, William, Dillard

and Arthur. They did not like the name Martin so decided to change it to Seymour. They came by covered wagon from Kentucky to Kansas where they home steaded. A man named Singleton was the organizer of the caravan of covered wagons and carried many groups of black people from the east to the west. This is interesting because I've heard of people who used other vehicles of transportation, such as trains and boats, but not covered wagon. Pop Singleton was not related to us but conducted the caravans for ex-slaves. It was dangerous for people to travel alone so they traveled in groups. My father lived in Kansas where his father had a ranch and twelve children. Then the Seymours moved to Colorado where my father met my mother.

I knew my grandmothers, but my grandfathers both died before I was born. I remember my grandmother, Morgan, very well. She was a teacher. She went to Rust Boarding School in Holling Springs, Mississippi. We wrote to ask her about her records but due to a massive fire, all records before 1940 had been destroyed. She taught in various counties in Mississippi, was a thrifty, energetic, enterprising person and her children were very much like her. My grandmothers lived into their 80's.

Henry Morgan went to Fisk and was a Fisk Jubilee singer. I have a letter stating he was a member in the choir. At that time, right after slavery, the children and young people had no focus. The schools, perhaps not colleges at that time, gathered the children along the country side, brought them in and taught them. Many churches and organizations did that. Fisk was one, another was Lincoln. Henry Morgan ended up in Fisk. He sang with them as long as they were in the United States, but when they went to Europe, he couldn't go because of financial and health reasons. So, he taught school for a number of years until my grandmother got a job in Jacksonville, Florida. He liked it there and set up a billiard parlor.

Rosa Morgan was very precise and exacting in speech, and in her work habits, very consistent. She insisted that we be the same way whether it be homework lessons or scrubbing the floor, it didn't matter. Her talk was very detailed and you couldn't take her away from the point. She was very different, never got ruffled or upset, demonstrated patience beyond belief. She could talk a long time about a small subject that you might finish in 15 seconds. It would take about four or five minutes for her to elaborate upon a small subject. She was extremely thrifty. However, she was very generous when she thought it was time to be generous. She was a very loveable person. The house always smelled of oranges and spice and good things. She owned many art objects that were very detailed.

On the wall I have a picture of the Seymour family on their ranch in Colorado in 1902. They had homesteaded in Kansas and owned a lot of land that they improved and sold. They came by covered wagon to Colorado Springs where they had a large ranch in the Black Forest area. They worked very hard, went into dairy farming and trucked the milk to town every day. They all worked together.

In the picture is my grandmother, grandfather, four men who were born in Kentucky, three girls who were born in Kansas, and only eleven children, because one child died in childbirth. There were two reasons why my grandparents chose to go west, I imagine, because of the stories they'd heard and the Homestead Act lured people.

My grandmother was living during the Depression, but my grandfather had died in 1920. I was born in 1921. My grandfather, Seymour, moved to the city and my father owned a ranch in Falcon, Colorado. He did very well, but thought it was lonely. So he bought a farm closer to town. Three hundred acres was a lot of land, but you needed a lot because they had to plant things six inches apart, in furrows, to give the plants a little more opportunity to thrive. You needed more area there to make a living then. Now you can do well with an acre and irrigation. They didn't irrigate.

My father stuck to farming but had many jobs. He worked in the city and did his farming at night. He had a cap with a light on it that they used in the mines. He had lights on the tractor to farm at night. We had dust years in the 30's and that's when things began to fail. 1929 was a marvelous year, but 1933 was very rough.

The Depression didn't hit me directly because my mother sewed, made money with eggs, churned milk and sold butter. It seemed that in those times there was a strong thread, very protective. Both parents worked hard. Yes, if there were hard times, the children didn't know it. There was also a closeness with your neighbors. Seems as if a person was in need, it was taken care of. If people needed a place to stay, they'd work for a month of two in exchange for room and board or a small salary. Sometimes there were women who had children. We were a kind of nursery for women who needed to work but had no one to keep the children. There were many people we were able to help and who were able to help us. My uncle was a minister so lots of people came to him for help. So he would send them to us. His name was Alvin Chester Morgan. He worked very hard at the Church of God and Christ; worked in civic centers, on the council and was political minded. He never went into politics, but did serve.

My grandfather's father was either head of a tribe or king of a tribe in Africa. My mother is the only one who ever told me this. I didn't have an opportunity to substantiate that but it seems he lost his wife when the baby was born, so he brought the child on a pillow to the Americans.

I had a sister in Chicago who moved with us to Middleville Village, Michigan, a small town south of Grand Rapids. Where in Colorado we were subjected to prejudice, especially riding on the bus, we came here to a kind of oasis and there, it didn't seem to be any. The people were so beautiful and so lovely that it changed my entire view of human beings. These were Caucasians but they didn't treat you like you were dirty. We were called names out west. You just learned to not hear or acted like you didn't hear it. But here you were treated like you were part of the family and you were accepted. We were the only black people in the village and they took us in with open arms and love. In the west you didn't have to do a thing, just appear and they acted as though they hated you.

My first year in school the superintendent wanted me to live in town so I wouldn't have to walk four miles every day. It was a marvelous experience living in the village. My whole world changed. I had wonderful teachers and the children were receptive. I had two younger sisters and one older sister. My older sister had children and we all went to school together. It was a very rich experience. We had an 80 acre farm and my mother grew fruits and vegetables like I'd never seen before. I felt it must be paradise. Everything was luxurious and we had great food; things we could never grow in Colorado. In Grand Rapids there were far more black people than in any place I'd ever lived. You didn't get to know them easily. They were selective and you had to prove yourself before you were accepted. My father held on to part of the land in Colorado, sold it in the 50's and died in 1977 at the age of 92. He traveled right up until the last.

I went to school in Kalamazoo, then got a job in Ypsilanti teaching, and then came to Detroit. I was assigned to Russell school. The first day I walked right past it. It was different. The doors open up right on the street. I had never seen a place that didn't have a playground or swings. It was quite a different environment. I had never taught 100 children at one time in double sections in the gym. The children were so nice. I thought they were naughty, but they were marvelous. I remember an incident with a young fellow by the name of Mark, a great big tall guy over six feet. He was standing in the hall and I asked him what he was doing there. He told me he was at his post. I said, "No you aren't. Come on, let's go to the office." I took his arm as we walked to the office and I said to Mr. Fine, the Principal, "Mark tells me he is at his post at such and such a place." I told him he wasn't. Mr. Fine said, "Yes, he was." I said to Mark, "I am very, very sorry." He said, "Of course." The children were very different. They not only had respect for the teachers, they had respect for themselves. Their parents expected them to obey, so it was very different then. You could talk to a group of children and they wouldn't get smart. There would be no confrontations like you see today. But we did great things in thirty three minutes. I was teaching first through the eighth grade and I have to give credit to Sue Goodson because I would not have believed that you could teach one hundred children at one time, but she showed me how.

We had everything snapping, just like clock work. The school was on the platoon system from Spain. They brought it to New York, then it came to Detroit and was all over the city. Other cities, like Ypsilanti had self-contained rooms where they didn't have children moving from class to class. I think it's better for the child to have one teacher. The teacher knows what's happening with each child and if you keep that child two or three years, then you really get to know them. But in Detroit, children went to different classrooms. In the afternoon they went to music, art and

57

about four other classes. That's how we had one hundred children moving from class to class.

What inspired me to become a music teacher was that we had very good music teachers in Colorado and I loved music. I loved the classics, dancing and geography. I also had friends and cousins coming out of school who couldn't get jobs.

The Carters and Sheltons all had to go back to the south to work. A male friend of mine never got work, had four years of college and ended up working on his father's trash collection business. During the 30's, teaching was the only thing I knew about that was an open job. Even in Grand Rapids you couldn't go to business college to be a secretary. It wasn't open. I knew black teachers who taught in Albion, Michigan, so I thought I had a better chance planning to be a high school teacher. I wanted to teach home economics, and a counselor at Western told me my chances would be better if I became an elementary school teacher. "The south is going to employ their own first and you would be competing against many southern people. You will have a better time getting a job in this state teaching elementary school." I went home and told my mother he was prejudiced, but she told me, "No, he's telling you the truth." I usually listened to my mother because what she said usually was true down to the line. I changed my major from high school to elementary school teacher.

I wrote Tips Off The Old Block, because the family permitted me to have the family pictures. I told them, "If you let me have these pictures, I will write our history." It was a commitment I wanted to fulfill. After I got into writing the book, I said, "We need this for our children." I only wanted to write about the past. The proofreaders said, "This book isn't finished. We want to know what the chicks did." I said, "I can't go into all of that, if it's too many children." They wanted to know about their education and what they were doing. So I agreed to do a sibling tree and just write down when they were born, their education and employment. That was as much work as writing the book because I didn't know I had so many relatives.

Albert S. Rosemond (center), with staff congratulating Gov. Franklin D. Roosevelt on his nomination for President of the United States.

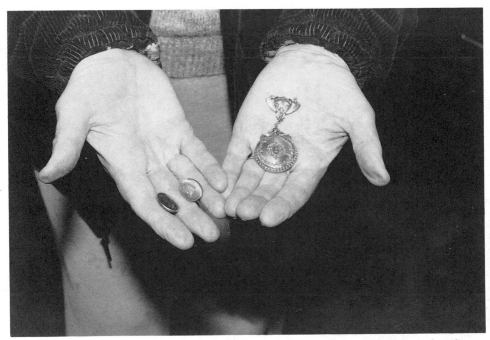

Treasured keepsake/Rev. John Forsyth's parents wedding gifts to each other

Viewing the Victory Garden

Birthday celebration in the 40's

Jim Ramsey still running at 80 plus   Can you name this car?

John Luster with Bayard Rustin

Winters in Detroit haven't changed

Polly Johnson in her lovely garden

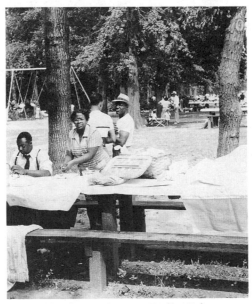

Summer fun at Belle Isle

Can you remember V–Mail?

MARY MARTIN REMEMBERS THE FIRST NAACP DINNER AND TEACHING AT MOORE SCHOOL FOR BOYS

I came to Detroit in 1946 and I lived in the Boston-Edison area. As I drive through there, today, I see so many houses where old friends used to live, and that brings back memories. There was Dr. Salisbury. My husband was a physician, so I knew a lot of the doctors, and I was often in and out of their homes. Now, when you go by the Constables home on John R and Arden Park, Dr. and Mrs. Constables are gone, Rosa Gragg is gone, Diggs is gone and Dr. Germany Bennett is gone. Dr. Salisbury had Kirwood Hospital; there was Dr. Burton, and then there was Prophet Jones who used to live there on Arden Park; there was Haley Bell, Todd Anderson, A.D. Henderson and his wife, Bertha. They were very dear friends of mine; and Arden Park looks like a ghost avenue now when I drive through there. I point the houses out, and I say I've been there, and I've been there, and I look to see these people. Dr. Burton, of course was one of our dearest friends, because he offered so much help to us as a young married couple when we came to Detroit. And then as I go on down I miss Haley Bell. We used to go in and out of his home. And so it goes back to many memories of fine people that I used to know.

Perhaps you could remember some incidents that happened during that time.

I was at the first NAACP Freedom Fund Dinner that was organized. Al Thomas, Jr., was one of the founders; and then, my dear friend, Dr. Lionel Swan whose birthday is on the first of April; and he is celebrating a monumental age. Dr. Swan was also instrumental in getting this dinner off the ground, and at that time, I think it was $100 per couple and people came in droves, dressed up in their finest clothes. They had entertainment by Billy Ekstine, Sammy Davis, Jr., and challenging speakers who were very good. That was an event that we looked forward to.

Where was that held?

It was always held at Cobo Hall, and at that time, they served strip steaks. The dinner was as good as the speakers! Baked potatoes, vegetables, nice dessert. Now the dinner is incidental because it seems most of the food was donated, and then written off. I think that back then, they didn't have the expertise of having someone underwriting the dinner, so a portion of the money was spent, and that was years ago. The dinner was exquisite. Everybody looked forward to the delicious meal.

What about your schoolmates, friends from church, friends of your mother or father? Let's go back to the schools then.

Well that'll be something to talk about. A lot of the schools have been demolished. The buildings are non-existent.

I know Eastern High School on Mack and East Grand Boulevard is torn down.

I used to be a school teacher in Detroit for 10 years, and I had the pleasure of working in one of the oldest schools in Detroit, known as the Riverside School. It was on 23rd. Street, near the Ambassador Bridge. They had a large enrollment of Spanish/Mexican children. Every Christmas we'd have a large Pinata hanging from the ceiling, and Mexican festivities. Everyone dressed in Mexican garments. The little

Everyone dressed in Mexican garments. The little children were so lovely. Because their parents didn't speak English, they children would translate, and it would be up to the teachers to try to relate what was going on, and what they were learning. It was quite an experience.

And then I had the pleasure of working at the Moore School for Boys, which is now extinct. That was really an experience. It was for "bad boys," but the principal was in charge. He used to come to the assemblies and say: "I go to the gym everyday to work out, so I'm ready to take-on any one of you fellows". I was a librarian. There would be six or seven boys in a class, and maybe two or three of them wouldn't come, so you'd have about four. Books were the last thing they wanted to hear about. They would be sprawled out and asleep, so I had to find some way to get to these boys. I decided I would get books that had guns, like Matchlock Gun, Treasure Island, and Pirates; books that had some intrigue that I thought would interest them. But I found that you had to be on your guard all the time, because they would be looking at you from head to toe looking at your jewelry. "How much did that cost?"

They used to line the boys up to catch the bus about 2:45 or so, and if you got too close to the stairway, they would automatically run against you and brush you this way or that way. So we learned to stand back, 'cause if you didn't, they would do it on purpose. Getty was there when I was there . It was quite an experience. They don't have that school anymore. Riverside was torn down. There is a bus depot there now for buses going to Canada.

What about the parents?

Well, you never saw the parents of those boys. They came from all over the city. They were all older

62

boys. They were really hard to work with. You had to find something to really maintain their interest. You had to find some alternative to reach them.

I've noticed a lot of controversy over certain books.

Well, in any library, even today, you have to get the children so involved. It's up to the librarian to promote it. If you can sell it, they'll buy it, or read it, but if you're passe, then they will be, too. If I had children, I never read stories. I would make books "talk", show pictures. I often had kindergartners and I could tell a story in such a way that their eyes never left me. If I found that their minds were wandering, I would cut it off, but, if they were paying attention, I let it go on and on and on. So that's a trick of a trade; something that you learn to do. If you find children who do a lot of reading, it's because the librarian has pushed them and coerced them; or their parents did.

JULIA CLOTEELE PAGE REMEMBERS DR. & MRS. HALEY BELL AND SEGREGATED HOSPITALS

Unfortunately, they took the Literature Program out of Detroit Public Schools. That's really where so many of our youngsters became interested in reading. This morning, I attended the program at the Downtown Library, and there was a young lady there who is still in college, but she's ready to publish her second collection of poems. She attributed her interest in writing to the program they used to have in the public school system here in Detroit. There were just so many fine things that gave our children some cultural background.

For instance, I taught in the auditorium program for a number of years, and there you had the opportunity to expose children to the different facts of science, music, literature, arts & crafts and so on; things that would stimulate their imagination. Today, except for that "idiot box," children don't have anything to stimulate them. They don't get a chance to get encouraged to write until they are in the high school English classes, which is unfortuante.

I taught at the Balch School. We had quite an auditorium program at one time. Our children were introduced to the instruments of the orchestra, and musicians from the symphony and various other musical groups would come in and perform for them. The youngsters knew the four families of the symphony, and we would create a "mock" symphony of our own. J.L. Hudson used to let us borrow the instruments, and the children would make instruments out of cardboard, and paint them. They would learn something about composition, the design of various instruments. The kindergartners started off with percussion instruments. They couldn't always pronounce the names, but they knew that was the first family of the orchestra, and that that was where you picked up your rhythm.

I have the distinction of putting Diana Ross on stage for the first time. We put on the operetta, Hansel and Gretal, and she was one of the 14 angels coming down the walk with "when at night I go to sleep, 14 angels at my feet". I have some home movies we made of these kids going down the aisle. Her sister, who is now a physician, was Gretal, and the young fellow who played Hansel eventually became one of the interior designers for Cobo Hall and the Renaissance Center. We had an opportunity to expose children to some things that, today, our children are not given the opportunity to experience. I just feel so sorry for our children, today. Unless they are in a private school, or have a teacher who just takes the time away from something else, they are not exposed to things that children were exposed to 25-30 years ago. At that time, if a child was creative there was some place in the school system that would recognize and cultivate that creativity.

Now, while I'm running my mouth, I'd like to mention one of my dearest friends: I call her my "other mother". That is Mary Bell. Mary and Haley Bell,founders of Bell Broadcasting, WCHB/WJZZ. They are responsible for so many things that a lot of people are not aware of. Most people are not aware of the fact that had it not been for those two people and their broadcasting studio, Motown wouldn't have been anywhere, because Berry Gordy couldn't get the white stations to play the recordings, and you have to have air exposure in order to do anything as far as a record company is concerned. Bell was responsible for giving these young people the opportunity to get that kind of exposure.

65

Remember when they broadcast from Euclid?

Yes. When they were on Warren. Now, they still do lot of the broadcasting from WJZZ on East Grand Blvd. The other station is in Inkster, now, I'm told. Two people who really made a fantastic contribution to our community and to the world as far as giving young people the exposure. I am fascinated listening to that lady talk at her age. She is really something else! She's into everything! I was looking at some papers I'd dug out and she had me in stitches the other day. She says she's been on every board for any organization in the city of Detroit, except the "Ironing Board!" She's about 93 years old, now. She's miserable because she fell off a ladder doing something she wasn't supposed to be doing, and she broke her hand and ankle. She's in a wheel chair most of the time, now, and she's so disgusted about that. But a tremendous person. Her picture was in the Michigan Chronicle a week ago. She's an honorary member of the AKA Sorority. To get someone to talk about Mary Bell and Dr. Haley Bell would really be something. The family worked together at the studio, including their two daughters, grandchildren and great-grandchildren.

Yes, very definitely, in the 50's or earlier, you had to be close to your family or someone else's because that was your entertainment. You did things within the family group and the neighborhood group.

Then there's a lady some of you might remember, by the name of Beaulah Whitby, an old time citizen of Detroit. I remember when I was in college and she was the national president of the Alpha Kappa Alpha Sorority, and we used to look at her in awe. She was a beautiful woman, and made a beautiful presentation. I ran into her once at the World's Fair with these two little girls who she raised to be wonderful young ladies and the great-grands. Then, Ira Whitby, the brother. The Burtons founded Burton Mercy Hospital, where most of my children were born, because, back there in the earlier years, blacks could not go into white hospitals, and that's been since 1950.

So, there was a strong community?

Oh sure, very definitely. the YWCA on Adams played a tremendous part. They held conferences for the older boys and girls there, too.

I've been in Detroit since 1925 and I have heard that Black mothers were not allowed in white hospitals. I didn't believe it.

It's true.

I find that hard to believe.

It certainly was rare. I am one of the rare ones. I was born in Herman Kiefer Hospital.

My sister was, too.

If you had a white physician, they would take you in there. Otherwise, no. There was a family of doctors, the Bernsteins. When my younger sister and I were born, Dr. Bernstein got permission for Dr. H.E. to just stand there while my mother was delivering us. He could not practice. At that time, you had Dunbar Hospital, Edith K, Thomas, Boulevard General, Parkside and Kirwood.

Even though they had Ford's, and other hospitals, black mothers were not allowed in there?

No, unless you were admitted to the segregated wing at Ford. Last year, I had surgery on my knee at Hutzel (1989). Three days after my surgery, I was in terrible pain, and the woman I shared a room with was in real pain. I think she was very, very sick, very ill and giving the nurses and doctors a bad time. One day, one of the nurses came over to my bed and said, "Mrs. Jones, the lady next to you, her Rabbi is coming in to see her today. When the Rabbi comes, would you mind leaving the room and going down the Lobby until they're through?" I was speechless. I couldn't believe it. I said, "No. I'm not leaving my bed. I'm not getting up. If her family wants to draw the curtains, they can. But I'm not leaving the room." I told my doctor about it. He has never mentioned it to me. I don't know if he ever said anything about it.

The thing about it is sometimes it's not just racial conflict, but some people are just prejudiced against seniors.

I suggested they move her to another room, which they did. I remember when I was working at the hospitals, when the doctors got older most of them were Caucasian-they didn't want to be bothered with Dr. Johnson because he was older. A lot of the white physicians lived in the Boston/Chicago area, so they weren't far from the hospital. But I would call Dr. Johnson and his wife and tell them that they were getting ready to have "rounds" and he would rush to the hospital, and the other residents would wonder how he would be there. This man had given his whole life to the hospital, and when they felt he was too old to be effective, they just kind of brushed him aside.

I'd like to say that I was in town when Joe Louis was in his hey-day, which was before I was married. But he had a manager named John Roxboroug, and they lived a very flamboyant life; had gorgeous cars, a convertible. I used to listen to his fights because there was no TV and I remember when Schmelling got knocked out by Joe Louis. We were so excited! We just had a fit, almost a near riot, because we were so happy.

Joe Louis represented us nationally and worldwide. I was living in New York at the time and people were just embracing him. They would stop traffic following him. I was fortunate enough to interview his wife. Joe Louis had died and she was married to a lawyer, and I went to the airport to meet her. They had adopted five children, and she was trying to hold onto these children. But she didn't get the same reception, naturally. They did have this stretch car. She gave me a beautiful background about him, and I thought it was so wonderful that even in his later years he was still thinking of someone else. Even though he was ill at the time, and they were staying at the St. Regis Hotel, and she had people who admired him who were really sacrificing their time just to be there to see if they could be of some help to her. What I got from that interview is, once you are a hero, it's really lasting.

That's why it's so important for our athletes, today, to put out a good image for our youngsters.

Dave Bing, for one, is really contributing.

There are enough to be impressive.

And also the Keys family group, which works in the community.

Speaking of restaurants, the old Gotham Hotel. They used to have a restaurant on Sundays. It was located on John R., and it was a joy to go there and meet your friends. Everybody knew that you would come to the Gotham at least once a week. They had the best food and that was a meeting place for Detroiters of all ages and social status.

Another thing, when I came to Detroit, people dressed up when they went to church. Then, I wouldn't think of

69

going out without my gloves and my hat. I still wear a hat. It was a place where I thought it was one of the beautiful things about Detroit. People were very conscientious.

My husband says when he sees these blue jeans—we called them "overalls." -and only the "country" people in the city wore them, or wore them to work, only. Some people who worked in the factory would change their clothes before they would come out in blue jeans. Well, I resent having someone else's name across my behind. Free advertising.

I laugh and say I only have my own name; never was caught up in a designer. It was so nice when you would see a family together. **Perhaps you could tell us about that: how the family would go together to church. They wouldn't just spread and separate; they would go as a family group.**

Well, yes, more so then than now. I think you'll find there's still a great deal of family gathering in church, all sorts of children. People are grateful for good friends, and teaching that helps them to make their lives straight. It's a good thing.

So, the church, school, and the parents were sort of like one nuclear unit.

I belong to St. John's Presbyterian Church, and what I find is that it's the grandparents and the great-aunts who bring the children to Sunday School; not because the parents were not raised in church, but it seems that the parents take a vacation from church. Some parents, but not enough, bring the children to Sunday School or church.

For some of those parents it's an opportunity to have a vacation from the children.

I remember when mine were small, I would take them to church, and at that time it was a storefront church.

I didn't like the idea to help build this storefront church, and Pastor asked my sister and I if we would go over and help Paster Bryant because he was a young man and we were living on the west side. We really had to get the kids in. A lot of blacks were not too keen on a Lutheran church at that time, so we really had to go looking for parishioners. My husband would get the car on Sunday morning I think he was one of those who would have liked to take a vacation, but, of course, he couldn't, and I would have to go upstairs, dress the kids, take them and bring them back. It was really something. Prior to that, on Saturdays, my sister, her husband, myself and my husband would go to the church to clean it up. I guess, now, if you asked a member of the church to do that, they would think you're crazy. But the church really grew. My husband was very fussy about his car. His car was perfect. He kept it that way, and so, when they'd wet the seat of his car, he'd be so upset! But you know how kids are! But we had a common interest, and we worked together.

We have the young people really involved in the program, involved in the music in the church, participating in fundraising with various projects. We feel quite happy about the participation of our young families. Rev. Anderson, our associate pastor, really changed the Sunday-School program around at Plymouth. One of the things she insisted on doing through our Board of Christian Education was to make sure that the on the fifth Sunday, children worship upstairs with the families because kids need to know how to act when they are in the sanctuary, too.

Before, you would take your children with you to the main service, and then they would go to other programs.

Again, regarding Beaulah Whitby, there's a tape of her funeral service which wasn't like a funeral service at all, it was done so beautifully. Such fantastic tributes paid to her and the various things she has done in the community. Mel Ravitz was there, not scheduled to be there, but he and Mary Ann Mahaffey came to pay tribute to this fantastic woman who was such a diligent worker.

Mrs. Jones brought an album that she put together, relative to her brother, who was an artist. He made ink drawings of different parts of the Bible. He did an ink drawing for me, of the Three Wise Men which I framed and hung on my wall. This brother was our favorite and every Christmas he would come home and spend Christmas with us. When he died, it was heart-wrenching. While I was in his apartment, I collected letters that he received and pictures he had and I put them into an album.

This is something that in the year 2000 your offspring can look at and know about their heritage. There was a young man who was a photographer for the Free Press.

My parents were from the Caribbean and they settled in Canada in 1913, 1916. It was a struggle. Some of us were born in Montreal, and work was very bad, so my Dad and Mom came to Detroit in April of 1925. My parents were the best ever; tough as nails, so hard on us. We had to walk a chalk line. They stressed education, and those of us that were not receiving an education have no one to blame but ourselves. I have many fond memories of growing up and of my parents. They will live in my heart, forever.

That's a wonderful tribute.

Mrs. Hale, I'd like you to tell about when you first came to Detroit and how your husband was looking after you.

I came to Detroit in October of 1945. I was born in Louisville, Kentucky. Another girlfriend and I drove here with her uncle and aunt for vacation. We were supposed to have stayed at the "Y", at the Lucy Thurman. However, they didn't have a room, so we wandered around on Adams Street. There was this Carlton Hotel. My husband was on the desk. I was 21 and this was my first time really being away from home, so we were trying to appear as if we were ladies of the world. When we went to bed that night, we were so uncomfortable that we piled the suitcases against the door. Anyway, the next morning someone knocked on the door, and when we answered, it was Nelson, and he was bringing us styles and everything. There was something about him that I just trusted. So whenever I went out I would tell him where I was going. The fellas started teasing him, and after about three days, he said "You two look like nice girls. I would suggest that you get a room with a private family. This is what is called the Valley, and mostly show people and hustlers live down here." So he told us what papers to buy, and we found a place on the Northend. So when we left, he asked if he could come to see me and I told him yes. Well, I've always known how to cook, and I would invite him for dinner and everything, and he was the only fellow I dated. We dated for two years, and then were married; and we'll be married for 43 years.

I love that story because if typifies Detroit, even though it was a large city and sort of spread-out at that time, it showed you that although he was a stranger he was guiding someone in the right direction.

He knew that I was "green" even though I was trying not to act like it.

Then, too, people had rooming houses, or they took people in and it was usually through the church.

Even when we married, apartments were very hard to come by.

I'd like to mention one other name that most of you knew; Myrtle Gaskill. She wrote for the Michigan Chronicle, and I don't think there were many journalists before her time. She was A#1. Also, Gladys Hill. Gaskill went into detail about all the social activities of the blacks, the people in Detroit, wherever they were. You could keep up with your friends. Now the paper has more church news, sports and other things. It's still a wonderful paper. I think we should be proud of the efforts of Mr. Quinn.

MARY GRAHAM SPEAKS:

Mr. McCall was my mother's first cousin, and when I got out of high school they gave me a job down there. Today they call it "Gofor," but I did help him because he was blind, and he could type like a whiz. But I would do all the reading to him so he could type. My cousin, Victoria, who was his daughter, trained me about writing columns. I used to go to sorority/fraternity dances, and cover these for her, and she would report. That's how I met Myrtle and Gladys. I knew all of them. It was good training. So I got my first job with the county after I left business school in 1939 or 1940.

So were you inspired in anyway?

I enjoyed it. It was very interesting work

How many people were on staff then?

This was back in 1938; not a whole lot of people. Do you remember Russell Collins? Russell was writing the sports column. Rollo Vest, Bill Lane was on staff, there, Julie Boykin. This was the Detroit Tribune, another one

74

of the Negro papers; that and the Chronicle ran more or less together.

Before that they had the Beacon, and Tony Langston ran that on Beacon Street.

I remember the Amsterdam News, a New York paper. I used to get that so I could see what was going on. They were very educational, too.

You could identify with them!

Yes, that's right.

Cloteele, you were speaking of Plymouth Church. Do you still go?

Oh yes.

Well, you know, my mother and father were two of the founders of that church. Marshall and Fannie Graham and I were the first babies on the Cradle Roll in 1920. They started out on Antietam Street, a little building, which was the synagogue on Garfield and Beaubien.

We just had our anniversary celebration last November, and your parents were mentioned.

I talk to my aunt quite often, Clifton's mother. She's my only other living relative outside my mother's sister. I talk to her every other day.

Tell her, Mary Virginia. She'll know who you're talking about. How many people were there, then?

I don't know. That was 70 years ago. It's all in the church history.

We only have about three of the original members still around. No, Thompson's family (Carrie Lee), the Grahams, and Mrs. Pate, Harris; and Mattie Shannon and her husband, Joel. Ethel Crawford. She played the organ.

Next week: Getting Through the Depression.

This is great. This is what I wanted to record, so people will look back and be able to remember, and be remembered.

There are some things that no one mentioned, i.e., the Graystone. That was so much fun, going to the Graystone on Saturday night. The Railroad Station, Michigan Central, Dummy George's, the Elmwood Casino.

POLLY JOHNSON REMEMBERS THE GOLDEN RULE

I never had very much myself. The things I've gotten down through the years have been through others. So I always thought I owed the world something just as those people did. I always did the best I could for everyone . I always thought of the other person really before I thought of myself. I could manage myself, but would see others who looked as though they couldn't hardly make it; so I would always help them out in some way.

I lived here and I didn't have a sitter for my baby as people do today. She is at this point, 65 years old. Sixty-five years back, they didn't have nursery schools and places to leave a baby while you worked; so naturally it was the Depression and I had to work. This friend of mine would keep my child for me. She was about sixty or seventy. Two dollars a day was top wages then, although I used to do a few things in between, like go to people's homes and take their curtains, tie backs, and I enjoyed doing them. I did all kinds of things like that. Finally I decided I wanted to buy a house because I had rented a place on St. Aubin between Monroe and Lafayette and this person at that time didn't keep up their home like people do today; so I bought some wallpaper and painted. Then the guy raised my rent, and I couldn't afford to live there after I had decorated it. So I said this is the last time I would ever rent.

There were houses for sale all over, so on Lafayette near Chene, where the Farmer Jack Supermarket is now, I bought a ten room frame house for $800.00. I didn't have $800.00 I had $300 and the dealer wanted $400 down. I borrowed the other $100 from the people I was working for. To close that deal I paid $400 and then I wondered how I was going to make those payments with the salary I had, so I figured , I don't need a ten-room house, but that was the cheapest one I could buy. I rented out the rear for $17.00 a month, which was more than what I had to pay monthly. So I decided now I want this house to look modern, not just plan. I had everything taken out of the inside. It was really just like a new house when I finished it. I had a blue bathroom put in, had Hudson to come out and make draperies, and laid carpet on the floor and everything, and was feeling real good about it now. This cabinet here in the corner was one of the pieces of furniture that I had. I keep it as a keepsake. The couch and chairs were reupholstered by Famous and they told me the story about them losing it. I guess someone else wanted to buy them and there was nothing I could do about it. That piece of furniture is about sixty-five or sixty-six years old.

I stayed in that house for awhile and then had to pay the babysitter $2.00 weekly, which didn't sound like much. The lady who was keeping my daughter, her husband lost his job, so any little bit of money was a help. They got their lights cut off. I decided since I wasn't home during the day, I'd let mine be cut off and have hers turned back on; especially since she was keeping the child for me. She thought that was really something, but I always figured out which ever was the best way to do it, it was hard. I did whatever it took to survive.

The houses were so close together, the same house on Lafayette and Chene, and my friend had this telephone in her house. I didn't have a telephone, so she said, "No sense in you trying to get a telephone. We can use the same telephone." So she had a long cord put on it, and when I got a telephone call she would come to her bedroom window and call me to my bedroom window and hand me the phone. I would talk, and when I'd get through, I'd call her and hand her the phone back. Of course we still had parties and everything. We just shared and were happy. We even had formal parties, pooled the money, and had big parties, went to Belle Isle, a bunch of us. Two dollars each would provide a lot of refreshments.

I didn't know a lot of people in the neighborhood because I worked all the time, but did have friends and neighbors and always was a friend to anyone I could be. Church was a great inspiration. I belonged to one of the oldest churches in Detroit; Second Baptist Church on Monroe. I helped integrate this church. It's an old historic church where they had the Underground Railroad. The slaves came in there and they decided they wanted to integrate, so they got this white minister and his wife and kids. Reverend Macy was his name. I was for it, but a few weren't. I had a party to welcome him and to invite some of the other people in to meet him.

I worked with the American Cancer Society in 1972. My husband died with lung cancer, and I used to sit in the University Hospital where he had his surgery. I knew a doctor on the staff there that did a lot of cancer surgery, and I thought this would be the place to take him. I took him from Harper Grace on Meyers Road to Ann Arbor and lived there with him. I promised to stay there with him. I stayed for $75.00 a day, and used the money we had saved for retirement. Of course after that was all gone, somehow I still had checks coming. After he got to the place he had to have treatment, he went over to the Medical Center daily and I moved into the Y, and had to take a cab to the Medical Center. It was kind of rough. He asked how the money was holding out, and I encouraged him not to worry. I didn't dare tell him I didn't have any, and simply said to myself, "Everyone lives till they die anyway", so I didn't have to worry about it. Checks were coming in on the 30th of every month, and I managed the best way that I could. He was operated on in May and he died shortly after. He said, prior to his death, "There's something I want you to do when you feel better". I told him, "I'm never going to feel better, but what is it you want me to do? " "I want you to work with the American Cancer Society. You didn't know it, but they gave the supplies that your husband had, and I've made a memorial to the Michigan Cancer Foundation." I said I'd do it.

They turned my name in to Mary Finch, one of the doctor's wives out in Ann Arbor. She called me and thanked me for agreeing to be chairman for the City of Detroit. I said I don't know anything about Cancer. I only know that it took my husband, and I'll do what I can; but Chairperson, I don't think so. After a long talk I still didn't agree to do it. She said, "Well, we'll come to a luncheon Saturday at the Medical Center". I agreed, and she talked me into starting to work with fund raising and giving service to cancer patients. I started in the block where I live. So I asked all the people on the block, and had a doctor to come and speak and introduced them to this program I was starting up with AMC.

Where I was living was kind of bad. They said blacks have more cancer than anyone else, so I figured we needed it desperately in this vicinity . We organized a branch, the Butzel Center on Kercheval and it went on real well for 10 years. Then they felt they needed to make some cuts and they moved to Garden City.

Some people were confused as to the name change, to Polly Johnson Cancer Foundation, and not the American Cancer Foundation. Well, we as volunteers didn't want to go to Garden City, but wanted to stay here in Black Bottom. In 1976, we had a meeting and decided to stay together and reorganize. They named it after me since I was the founder of the other branch. I

80

was truly stunned, but was very happy it was going to continue. Every morning I would go to the Medical Center and encourage the people. It was painful to see people that sick and not be able to help them.

The best cure I would have for cancer is to treat it before it gets out of hand. I can see why black people have more cancer. We have less money. If a person has a cough or pain for more than two weeks, you need to see a doctor. And if that is done, a lot of cancer can be stopped before it starts. It doesn't start over night. However, most people don't try to treat it until it has grown. Some people seem to think it spreads due to operations. Not true. It spreads because of not being treated soon enough, or early detection signs not being paid attention to.

God is the only thing I've ever had to hold on to. My grandmother was the first one to instill religion in my life. We'd go to Sunday school, and stay for church service, go home and have your chicken dinner, go back to BYPU, and then stay for service that night, and that was you livelihood. That's all you knew. Your fun was to sing in the choir or make some speeches. That was really all I was taught. I never went to parties. I was only exposed to church. As a result of my church upbringing, it was inbred in me to do for others.

When I was young, I used to work for people. I didn't have an educational background, so I learned to cook, clean and the people I worked for would always have things to give away, which afforded me the opportunity to always have more than I needed. I knew people who would need, say a bedroom set or a dinning room set, or whatever, and I would always be able to tell them about it. I've always been able to have something to give, or information to help people with what they needed. That's where the old saying comes from, "You've got to know somebody who knows somebody". I also did alterations for people as well as had a Victory Garden. I shared the

81

produce with many who were less fortunate.

My mother always shared. She lived on a farm
in the country, or a plantation. They would kill these
hogs and give all the meat away. You had to, because
you didn't have deep freezers and if you wanted meat to
eat, you had to share the rest, because you couldn't eat it
all.

There used to be hobos, and my mother would
wash their clothes and give them extra clothes. They
were like the homeless of today. She would take them
in, make a pallet on the floor, on their way travelling
somewhere else. I guess you could say we practiced the
golden rule and felt that if we needed help we would be
able to get help, too. If someone would knock on the
door, and it was closed, you didn't even say, "Who is
it?" You'd just say, "Come in." In Detroit and other
cities, it was just like that.

I used to get up early in the morning and wash
my clothes and hang them on the line and go to work.
When I'd come home in the afternoon, take them in, or a
neighbor would take them in if it started raining.
Sometimes if I'd wash in the afternoon I'd forget about
them and they'd stay out there all night. You hooked
the screen door, and slept there all night with the door
open. Go out to Belle Isle, sleep waiting for a table, go to
the boat race. Now there's so much crime and drugs.
It's dangerous. Nothing like it used to be.

Being able to relate to those beautiful days, a
walk down the street was a walk down the street, even
at night in the dark by yourself. Going to the store
you'd never fear anything. If someone else was going to
the store, they'd offer to get you something, and you
could pay them later. I think you get out of life what
you put into it. Be concerned about what you're supposed to do, don't point fingers at others.

82

WINTER COMES EARLY UPSTATE IN NEW YORK

Snow falls unexpected, soft,
wet, yet warm, purest of white
flakes drift to the ground.

The light from the sun becomes a rainbow of color, then
the chill settles in.

Snow becomes glazed streets,
crisp, punchy beneath the feet.

Outside on winter days,
clothes dry stiff and hard, long
underwear can't warm frost-
bitten hands or toes, nor bring
a smile to taunt faces.

Going to school kids ventured
out on little hills, testing their
brittleness, and shortness of
breath.

Night drapes the skis, the
darkest of blue, stars appear,
the moon enjoys winter's
view.

Beyond, icicles dressed the
snow in white silver reflect-
ing light from the Hansel,
Gretel type houses.

Pot belly stove, children then
sleep underneath heirloom
quilts, sharing the last piece of
penny candy, logs for the fire,

and lumps of charcoal give
warmth.

Wet shoes and boots drying in
front of the stove, grown-ups
talking of colder days yet to
come, big chunks of vegetables
in soups and stews, morning's
cooked oatmeal, oozing with
butter, a choice of hot choco-
late or Salada tea.

Sleighs coasting faster, and
faster down steep hills, laugh-
ter, little ice crystals forming
on faces, the park expresses
winter's wonder.

Ice hockey for the male gender
skating on frozen pond, tobog-
ganing, skiing, ice sculpturing,
and just snow balling, the snow
banks, last, last, and lasted, till
time to take off winter's ga-
loshes.

Irene Rosemond

This typifies the kind of life we all shared,
feeling very self assured of families loving each other.
We had things to laugh about, and we had some things
that were sad, because those were the days before
penicillin and, so they were sad days, too. But most of
all with my reflections I have right now, there was a
feeling of love and people did not covet what another
person had. Then there was a tranquility of just genu-
inely being in a city or on a street where there was just
that warmth, and all ethnic groups that lived around
you or in the same vicinity, or even next didn't have a
feeling of hatred. We just got along and when someone
died, they came over to do whatever they could do to
help. They watched your house, although it wasn't
necessary when there was a death in the family because
there wasn't that pettiness to steal from your neighbor.

The biggest thing is you had fruit trees, and
some of the branches would be so heavy. The kids
would take some of the fruit, but come in my yard, very
congenial. They had the usual differences, but nothing
to say that you can't play with that child any more.
When you can't reflect on anything that was wrong, it's
hard to reflect on something that was good, because the
good happened every day. The most important thing
that happened in Albany was baseball, and I remember
my father owning a small minor league black baseball
team. They didn't have anyplace to dress because they
didn't have any gyms or lockers, and they weren't
recognized at that time. They would have to dress and
undress in the cellar or basement.

I remember one thing. My mother couldn't
cook, so I think I was the youngest kid on the block who
knew how to open a can of food with a can opener.
Most of the women cooked, but my mother sewed

85

extremely well and my father was the cook of the family. When he left Lexington, Virginia, he said that he was always going to see that his children were well fed because he was tired of the fact that when he was a young boy the minister always got the best. I have heard stories about how the ministers were; when they weren't paid salaries and they had to go from one family to another to be paid with a meal. That was the method of paying ministers a long, long, long time ago.

My father was an excellent cook, and he taught us all how to act in a restaurant. My mother also taught us the art of living well and the graces of good etiquette. Another enterprise my father had was Mrs. Irving's School of Grace. He sponsored her and all the young black kids in the neighborhood would go to Mrs. Irving's house on Saturday, and she would teach us how to play the piano, and how to dance the proper way. We had our usual teasing of each other, and then we would have a recital, and our parents were shown exactly what we had been taught. I don't think they have schools like that now. Perhaps they call them Finishing Schools. We were taught how to act in public and how to sit. It was one of the first times that we were all exposed to the classics. In a way our parents and friends were really formulating us to be the best that we could be in whatever we chose in life.

Back to Detroit; when I got here in the middle to late 30's, Detroit was a very nice place to live and if you were black you were limited as to where you could live. I remember the excitement when there was an apartment on Leicester and it had just been turned over to blacks. My sister, her husband and myself lived there, and we were so excited because we thought this was the place to be, Detroit being as it was. King and Josephine Streets, and the west side were really the choice places to live. They had the trolley cars. It was six cents to ride and one cent for a transfer. That was funny because I'd

come from the Bronx where there were subways. I
adapted very easily to Detroit, and I remember that
people were in a state of shock because I had two fur
coats. Usually the people who wore fur coats were
people in the Numbers rackets. Many people said, "Do
you work for the numbers" I said, "No," and they said,
"Well these coats that you've got." I said, "Well in New
York, it's different. It's cold there, and it's no big deal
having more than one fur coat." That was one of the
most amusing things to me. I don't think they ever
believed me, but who cares. Jobs were hard to get then.
I worked for Dr. Matthews, a pharmacist whose wife is
still living. I worked in their drug store. Then I got a
call to go back to New York. I stayed awhile and
worked in my trade as a window trimmer. I came back
to Detroit and worked for my brother-in-law who had
started an accounting service. I worked for him for a
couple of years and met some very interesting people,
my future husband included.

Detroit at that time, down in the Valley, it was
delightful. The people who were involved in their
businesses in the Valley ranged from places to eat to
numerous other kinds of establishments. Everyone was
friendly, people were very congenial. Of course there
were the do's and don'ts but all in all it was very warm.
I think what you give to a city is what you get out of it.
Down in the Valley, as they called it, if someone would
take something of yours and you would say, "Stop,
thief!" everyone would run and catch the thief. I
remember that happened once when I had a fur coat
taken from me when I was in one of the show bars down
there. I said, "Someone's taken my coat," and they all
ran after him, and retrieved it. I said that would not
happen in New York city.

There were some other incidents where they
made a very big show of feeling. There was this singer,
a local singer who was trying to make it and it was a

place called the Three Sixes. It was sort of elegant for the city of Detroit, and people were very supportive of local talent. I remember when I first came to Detroit, I had never seen so many cars in my life, because the average person in New York took the train downtown to Manhattan or the subway or the "L." When I got to Detroit I thought it was a parade. They said, "What are you talking about? Look at all the cars parked on the sides of the street. They belong to the people on the block." I said, " You've got to be kidding. What about those cars there." They said, "That's my next door neighbor's car. They all work at different places and so they each have their own car." That to me was most impressive - all the cars in Detroit.

Another thing I fell in love with were the trees in Detroit. They were so beautiful. Every street had trees, trees, trees and more trees. Coming from the Bronx, trees were few and far between. You had to go to the city parks to really enjoy nature. Detroit always represented a city of trees.

MR. JAMES T. JENKINS REMEMBERS THE GRAYSTONE BALLROOM

I was fortunate enough to pass the exam for Transportation Equipment Operator for the City of Detroit which was called Bus Driver. So in 1941 I was hired as a bus driver and for 32 years I worked with the Transportation Department and I was always around music. I was always at the Graystone, always at the Flame, at the Garfield Lounge, in the Paradise, Club B & C which was changed to the Club El Cino and also the Three Sixes, and Sportrees. All the clubs where there was music, dancing and pretty girls, you could always find me. And over the years down into the mid 1960's I joined the club called Men Who Dare. They gave scholarships for under-privileged people. They gave those scholarships to help get young people into college and get them "in the door." We started giving little dances at halls, and we grew and grew until we finally went to the Light Guard Armory on East Eight Mile Road and Ryan. So to go to that kind of auditorium to have a fund raiser, you should have a national band. I guess that was in the late 60's when I was lucky enough to start promoting and bringing bands like Basie, Woody Herman, Duke Ellington, Thad Jones and Mel Lewis, Super Sax. We had all kinds of bands out there raising money.

Then it was just the people of the 1930's and 1940's who remember the grand times and the Big Band Era and the Graystone Ballroom. That is how I got connected with the Big Band System. Count Basie was staying at the Fort Shelby Hotel and he was leaving one morning and I was trying to catch him to get him to commit to play for a fund raiser for me. He gave me his itinerary, and suggested that I talk to the New York booking agency. Gave me the phone number and I was off and running. I was with the Big Time.

One of my favorite spots over the years was the

great Graystone Ballroom. It was a beautiful castle. It was limited to Blacks on Monday night and midnights on Thursday nights. It was just as grand on those nights as it was when the white people went there on Friday, Saturday or Sunday night. To think about what you would put on! You put your "soup and fish on". You couldn't go like the kids go to dances now. If you couldn't have your best or, if it was one suit or one pair of shoes, you had it shined and cleaned or you pressed it yourself, so you could enter that beautiful palace, glide over that dance floor. You danced and your feet never got tired. Then you would glide out the doors to the garden where you would dance under the stars from ten to twelve. Then inside from twleve to two. They would have two bands. They would have the "battle of the bands" and you would never quit dancing. When one band quit the other would strike up.

Rudy Valley played there on Easter Monday night in 1934. Fifty five hundred people came. The original bandstand had to be closed off and they had to build a portable bandstand across the front of it because when it was built in 1922 the big bands then were about ten or eleven pieces, maybe twelve. But in the late 20's and early 30's, the band grew to sixteen, seventeen pieces. They had to build a portable stand that would hold a piano, and a seventeen-piece band and two singers, male and female. There was always two hundred to three hundred people standing in front of the bandstand. They were listeners; they didn't dance at all. They just stood there and applauded and always recognized the great soloists and the people who played piano, and soloed on the drum, sax, trumpet or whatever it was. You had the dancing people. You had the people who went up in the balcony that overlooked the dance floor that had the big glass ball that would rotate. They would turn the lights down and the mirrors would silhouette all over the ballroom. It was just like you were in a fantasy castle.

There was the refreshment bar at the front that served cokes, milkshakes and hot dogs, and the little nook you could go in with your girl and get close. They brought the Chick Webb Band one summer night. There was a beautiful moon, dancing under the stars and Ella Fitzgerald was singing "Let's Build a Stairway to the Stars." It was just one of those numbers that made her famous. The culture today and the respect for the great music and the people who played it, and the foundation that was laid that this music we listen to now is built from. It doesn't get its recognition, but jazz, blues, and religious church songs will live on.

The Graystone closed in the late 1950's, and Berry Gordy, who was the founder and president of Motown Records, bought it and was going to build one of the greatest night clubs in the middle west. He was so popular at that time he could have gotten any part of Detroit that he wanted, because everyone looked to Motown, because it was another Beal Street, or Rampart Street. Maybe if he had taken Paradise Valley, we could have had a revival because Paradise Valley was the Harlem to Detroit until urban renewal, expansion of commerical people and the building of the Chrysler (1-75) freeway destroyed it. After Berry Gordy bought the building and had everything he needed, he opened it only for private parties. Then he had starlights in his eyes, and he wanted to go to California to make movies. He just left and left everything open to the vultures, and scavengers who broke in and just tore it up and took everything that they could sell, and started a living quarters in it. In the cold weather, they started building fires in it. The fires burned up the beautiful dance floor and the bandstand and then it got so bad that the firemen had to cut holes in the roof to flush the fire out and nobody tried to cover the roof. Then the elements and the pigeons came in. I was told by some of the Motown people that the building and safety were so bad and hard on them, they were told they would have to close it up or tear it down.

That's when the Graystone Jazz Museum was formed. Duke Ellington had just died, and we needed a memorial someplace to have this history, to have this culture. At first you thought just to have an International Museum Jazz Hall of Fame, but the few people who gathered around said, "Why can't we ask Motown for the building and become a tax exempt status, and they can write it off as a donation to our non-profit status?" A committee met with the Motown people and they advised the committee that they should become a viable organization with a Federal Exempt status, and they might consider it. It took a little time to get the Federal Tax Exempt status and then when we got that we went back to Motown with our 501(c)(3). Then I was told that they couldn't make the decision. It had to be made in L.A., and they couldn't recommend it to L.A. They had a CPA handling Motowns affairs. He was in the Town Center in Southfield, so I called this man, and he never heard about Graystone or anyone trying to save the building. He said the building wasn't for sale, but we could put a proposal together and he would send it to L.A. In the meantime, Coleman Young had become mayor and president Gerald Ford had been appointed president after the resignation of Richard Nixon. He allocated $600,000,000 toward the building of the subway for Woodward Avenue. When that was announced, everyone who had property on Woodward Avenue saw dollar signs.

It was on the proposal that maybe Canfield would be a stop for the People Mover. Motown thought that would be more valuable as a lot than trying to just tear the building down, or just give it to somebody. They went to a very expensive demolition group, and thought one wrecking ball would do it, but the building was so sturdy they had to bring another wrecking ball to demolish it. So as a small, non-profit oranization scuffling, trying to get artifacts and everything, we were able to save some of the artifacts that were in the ballroom.

My biggest disappointment was the sign that used to hang on Woodward Avenue that said Graystone, which was on the third floor. It's probably someplace out in a landfill where they dumped all that stuff. That was 1980. We have been trying to prove that our vision and mission can become a reality. Since we couldn't save the ballroom, we felt we could have a jazz museum. In the last seventeen years, we have been working on this.

The whole idea came after the death of Duke Ellington, in May 1974. I had the pleasure of booking Duke Ellington at the Light Guard Armory that February and we gave a special award to him. He couldn't attend the award giving, which was held at the Ten Gentlemen on John R and Milwaukee. It was a luncheon. Unfortunately, he was very sick at the time, so he sent his son, Mercer, and whenever they played for the dance that Saturday at the Light Guard Armory, he brought a substitute piano player to relieve him. He loved the public so. He would come out and play every 15 minutes, then he'd go back in the office where we had a couch that he would lie down on. Of all of his autographs, Cootie Williams took that honor. He was the lead trumpet player in the Duke Ellington band, and he sat on the bandstand and signed autographs for the people. We were lucky enough to get Ford Motors to donate a courtesy Lincoln Town Car to transport Duke and Mercer around during the time they were here. At that time the Statler Hilton Hotel on Washington Boulevard was open and that's where they stayed.

We had posters left over from that promotion. At that time I was promoting for the Men Who Dare, which was a scholarship organization. I retired in 1973 from the City of Detroit as a bus driver, and had a job in

Ann Arbor as Transportation Counselor. I commuted there, daily. I'd received a Christmas card from Duke Ellington, prior to that, which made me reflect back to a conversation the night he played for us at the Light Guard Armory. He told the young lady he was with to mail some cards. So she did. I commented to him that Christmas had just passed. He explained he never sent his Christmas cards out until May so they didn't get hung up in the mail or Christmas rush. This was February 1974, and in May I received his Christmas card. I still have it. Three days later I was driving on the freeway and it came over the radio that Duke Ellington had just passed. That's when my wheels began to spin and I felt we should have some kind of recognition, because he was so great and there should be some kind of memorabila to these great musicians. I thought the Graystone should be the place where these items should be housed.

Bands that didn't play at the Paradise Theatre played at the Graystone; like the McKinney Cotton Pickers. They were the first black band to play at the Graystone in 1926. How they got in there, was they were playing at a club in Toledo, Ohio. The booking agent had bands all over the midwest, had orchestras on the steamers going to Buffalo, Cleveland, Cedar Point, Wisconsin. Someone told him he should hear them. So he invited them to come to Detroit, and wanted to put them in the Arcadia Ballroom. When they arrived, he decided to put them in the Graystone, instead. They were the first black band to play in the Graystone. He changed their name to the McKinney Cotton Pickers. Dave Wilburn who was the last of this group, told me this story. Dave gave me a lot of people, internationally, who joined me in trying to save the Graystone. They didn't like that name because they didn't pick cotton. However, this was the stigma that was given blacks at that time. They decided that since they were only going to be here for two weeks they would deal with the name and go back to their original name when they left. That two weeks lasted seven years. They became internationally known, went all over the world, were recognized, and the name still stands today.

His son is a guard over here at Grand Circus Park. He came by and brought me some of the pictures we already had. He doesn't remember too much about his Dad. Everyone is mostly gone, or too old.

The Graystone Museum started in 1974 at 716 Lothrop in a little room ten by ten, if that big, and it was only an idea. As offices became vacant, we rented them, but I was able to get a reasonable rate due to being part of the bus drivers' union. In 1980, they tore down the building and everyone left me. I wanted to pursue building a jazz museum. I was the only board member left. I finally found enough people to believe in our comeback, received $500 from the Detroit Council for the Arts immediately after Mayor Young was elected. The biggest grant came when I convinced the Michigan Council of the Arts that we were a worthy organization and had a pilot program they should support. They gave us $15,000, so I set up a procedure for accounting for this money. I got an accountant, John Gray, and everything was accounted for, adequately. We have support, inquiries, visitors from as far away as Russia, South America, China, Europe, all over the world. Now from Siberia. We hope this will continue to grow and be a grand tourist attraction. We desire to have our own wing in a building with the Museum of African American History, a library, gift shop, viewing room. We're still collecting artifacts, memorabila. We hope the younger blacks will not throw away their parents' old things, thinking it's junk, but will donate to continue our heritage.

1521 Broadway is the headquarters. The theme is to show what the music was and how it travelled, how it started. Jazz is an African American experience, founded, probably, before Christ, in Africa, and when the slaves were brought over to America, they landed in the Southern Mississippi, in New Orleans. These people were brought over here and their art and all their culture was left in Africa.

We want to show the theme, how it came about, where it went, how it grew and has sustained itself through the years, how it was discovered, who were the great people that presented it to us. Scott Joplin was one, Jelly Roll Mortin, King Oliver, Louie Armstrong. Right now, we have displays from the late 1800 up to 1991. We are now trying to introduce to the young blacks their great role models, to show when the white man was living in caves we had great kings and queens in Africa and great warriors like Hannibal who came across to conquer Rome, and all these different people. I don't know what this captialist theme is today. However, they don't want to accept this music or support it, or expose it to the young people.

I have gone out to the schools, as well as have tours come here. These sophisicated kids are interesting. I introduce myself, and in so many words, I say you don't even know who your role models are. When I ask them who was Josephine Baker was they can't tell me. Who was Scott Joplin, Louie Armstrong? They don't know. This is what we're going to have to do about our history, our culture. Let them know to be proud that they're black, let them know to have pride, that they have these great people in their ancestry. I have the whole Paradise Valley set out, every joint, every bar, every home. All I need is money to put it on a mural, because how can these kids know how great Paradise Valley was if there is nothing here for them to see? All they can hear is what their grandmother and grandfather tell them. The worst thing to happen to us was the Civil Rights voting of 1964. It killed everything. All the little nightclubs, black hotels, soul food restaurants. Where do you go now? We used to go to the Pelican, or Fergusons, Lark. Bob Holloway couldn't read a lick,

96

couldn't spell his name but he owned the Lark, and had the biggest lunchroom down stairs, and a dinning room upstairs, and had real linen napkins. If you don't tell these kids these things, how would they know? You want to go to the library and ask for the Hackley Collection. They have it locked up. The best thing is I have never gotten hate mail saying "you don't know what you're doing down there."

John Luster Remembers the Trade Unions and Family Support

My name is John Luster, I'm 65 years old and was born on April 8, 1927, in a little town called Hernando, Mississippi, about 17 miles south of Memphis, Tennessee. The significance about that date and that time and that place is that I was born into a totally segregated society. I can remember in 1933 and 1934, we didn't have highways, electric lights, nor running water. It was mostly farming area. Everyone was poor and I remember that too. In 1933 and '34 was when they began to build federal highways through Mississippi, and that caused a great change. People rented mules and horses to work on building roads. I was just six or seven years old, but can remember it just as plain as if it was yesterday. Although society was clearly separated, I think it's important that we record these memories because it was against the law for Blacks to have newspapers or receive them in the mail, or have them in their home.

My grandparents owned their own land. Consequently my brother and I and all my family were fortunate enough to have material things. They were farmers, raising cotton, corn and vegetables. They were also truck farmers. They would go to the market and try to sell their goods. When they couldn't they would go door to door in Memphis, and we would trade those off for different things. My grandmother was a school teacher and had a great love for knowledge and education. If she couldn't get any money she would trade old clothes, newspapers, magazines, books, etc. I loved reading. She was the only school teacher in that county, and school only lasted about three or four months. The overseer would come and tell the parents they had to take their kids out and bring them to help farm, or move. So half of the four months there were very few people in school. Only about three or four kids were able to stay in school for four months. So that's some of the memories about growing up.

I lived in town with my mother and four brothers. We would go out and visit our grandparents and stay with them because my mother worked as a cook in Hernandoz for the local banker and they weren't really paying her a lot of money; only about $2.00 a week. With two kids, she had to pay rent, buy coal oil, etc. , so usually in the summer time my brother and I would go to the farm and stay.

I attended elementary school later on in a little town in Hernandoz, and that's kind of an interesting story, too. I think about kids now and the things they do, and we have great concerns about them. There was a controversy over the public school that lasted 50 or 80 days a year, that the public school had a reputation of being bad. It was all Black, and the kids were fighting. My mother didn't want my brother and I to attend that school because she was fearful that we would get hurt, so she arranged for us to go to a private Baptist school. There were only about three or four children, but even there among the Blacks, I became aware of racism.

Most of the Blacks there were light. My brother and I were brown skinned, but there was a bias within that school system. One of the young ladies attending was the daughter of a teacher who taught in the public school. These are all Black, and the teacher played favoritism. Since we were the poorest ones there, poorly dressed, we'd end up experiencing displeasure from the teacher. The other kids would accuse us of pulling their hair, or hitting them, and the teacher would always punish us whether we did it or not. When the kids found out they could get away with doing this, they kept doing it.

One time a little girl accused me of pulling her hair, and the teacher said, "Come on, stick your hand out." She had a switch, and to this day, I still have that knot in my hand as a result of that whipping. I made my mind up right then, but I wasn't going to tell my mother. I decided I was going to go back to public school. My brother and I agreed that the next Monday, we were going to go and enroll ourselves in the public school, and that's what we did. I found out the kids over there were just the same, even though they were the same kids we had been playing with for years. I wasn't afraid of them. We had been attending school an entire semester before my mother found out. We had saved the money we were supposed to pay every three months. When she found out we were going to public school, had not gotten beat up and got her money back, she was pleased. That experience stayed with me a long time, and I began to appreciate learning and education and access to education even more that I had prior to entering that kind of environment.

In 1937, I got a job, was enrolled in public school with my brother, and again my mother didn't now anything about it until I went home and told her. I worked in a little grocery store after school every day and on Saturday in Hernandoz. I started earning seventy five cents a week. Later on I changed jobs, learned to drive, went to work at a Chinese grocery store. I was 11 years old. I learned how to drive at that age. Back then everything was really different, and the only person able to issue drivers license was the highway patrol. They would come into town once a week, pass out drivers licenses to local business people. They would go and get them for their kids and their workers. So that's how I got my drivers license. I didn't even go. The Chinese store owner filled out the application and made sure it was taken over to the highway patrol. So I learned how to drive in 1937 on the Chinese store owners papers.

It was a 1939 Ford, and after he was sure I knew how to drive he said he'd raise my wages, and we would drive up to Memphis and buy meat, come back and cut it up and sell it on Saturday. Every Friday, after dark, I would drive to the packing house in Memphis, Tennessee, because you weren't supposed to bring fresh meat into Tennessee without a permit. I'd go to the stock yards every Friday night, buy a couple of hogs and half a cow, bring it back, and we'd cut it up and have it ready the next day. We didn't have ice boxes, so it wouldn't last very long. That's the year I got my social security card, and I've had some kind of job every since. When I retired in 1989, I sent in to the Social Security Administration for my record, and I never missed a quarter from 1939 to 1989. I had earned something in every quarter from that time to this. I was surprised because I thought some of those years I had not earned anything, but I had, according to official record.

My mother had been married twice before 1939. That year, she married a young chap. This young chap was my step-father. His name was Henry Taylor Williams, and he changed my life forever. He had a profound affect on my life. He was one of the wisest men that I'd every met, and I learned so many things from him. I learned how to love, how to be concerned about other people's feelings, and how to examine my own feelings. Of all my relatives, my step-father had the most profound affect on my life. He was just an out-standing person. He always encouraged me to read, be honest, respect other people, taught me how to handle fear, to learn how to listen. He was the first person that I had become aware of who had dealt with fear. You know we all have different fears, but he was an individual who had learned how to manage it, and that always fascinated me. We were as close as two human

101

beings could be.

Relative to my grandmother, she had a great impact on me also. She used to take me to Sunday school. She'd go to church two or three times on Sunday and sometimes during the week. She was a very religious person, very active in the church. People had an enormous amount of respect for her. She was always a leader, she was approachable. So even though she was the only teacher there in the county, everybody loved her, and they called her Miss Vicky. I'd also go to the market with her. She was a peddler. We'd buy candy from Memphis and baking powder, everything you could use in the home, and we'd walk for miles around to all the farms, trading things. She always encouraged me to read, write and figure, so that was one of the reasons I was able to get a job at the grocery store, because I had learned how to count early.

Almost no one could read. Most Blacks back then, not only could not read, but had more difficulty in indicating that they couldn't read. So it wasn't just that the Whites were discouraging them from advancing; they didn't see a need for it. If you spoke their language correctly and could read and write, you couldn't get a place to stay. Part of the reason for that was the sharecroppers had to turn back part of what they produced, cotton, corn, etc. in order to have a place to live. So if you could count, they couldn't cheat you. They could always find people who couldn't read or couldn't count. When people would indicate that they could read and write, they would say, "Well you go and find someone who is impressed with someone who can read and write because we don't need you." Inspite of that, my grandmother encouraged us to learn to read and write.

We would go and visit people, and we would sit down and talk about what we had to offer. Usually, when someone was going to buy, I'd have a little piece of paper and have it already figured up and I'd hand it to her. Most people would say, "No, you figure it, that boy can't count. Who ever heard of anything like that?" The point I want to make is I enjoyed that. I was impressed by people knowing I could read and write.

On Sunday, I wanted to play with the other children, but I can remember some of the other sisters on the way home from church. The men folk would come near the church, but not come to the church. They would be in the bushes shooting craps and drinking, and I remember the sisters saying, "Isn't that a shame? They come that close to the church and won't come in. They ought be be horse whipped." I can remember my grand-mother saying, "No, Sister Jones, they love us, and we love them, and we have to pray for them. We don't want to hurt them." I couldn't understand that then. Later on, I did.

Things got tough economically in '40 and '41. There was even a lay-off at the grocery store. This was just prior to the war. My step-father couldn't find work, so in '42 he took me to Memphis, Tennessee, to Booker T. Washington High School and enrolled me, and he went to work at the cotton yard. We got a room and he and I lived together. I went to school, and three or four weeks after we'd been there, he said he'd gotten a job. That was the first of many jobs that he got farming. He went back to the school then and arranged for me to leave school at twelve o'clock everyday, and then go to the cotton yard at 2 p.m. We worked there for about four months, trucking these big bails of cotton. So I worked and went to school, and it was a different world. It was the first time I wasn't in a one-room school, and they had Algebra, English, History, and all the other classes. We saved money out of what we were making every two weeks, and sent money back home to my mother.

In '42, the war was gearing up and there was this

103

textile company, American Finishing Company. I still have my badge from there, and my membership in the credit union, and my membership in the Textile Union. That's when I became interested in the union. That's the year I was introduced to A. Philip Randolph. He was coming into Memphis and my dad took me to hear him. They had been talking about him coming to Memphis six months before he got there, and everytime they would agree to a church he was going to be at, Cronk's stooges would put pressure on the minister and he would have to cancel out. None of the mainline churches would take a chance on allowing him to speak in their facility, so I first heard him in a little store front. He, too, had a major impact on my life.

I had never heard any human being use correct English and speak with the eloquence that he did, White or Black. I would ask my dad ,"Why is he calling people Black?" I'd never heard that expression. But he was talking about White and Black workers, talked about the masses. My dad is one of those union fellows who worked with John L. Lewis. I knew then I wanted to be a trade unionist. I told my dad I wanted to know more about the union. He said, "Be careful, don't do it on the job, but keep on doing it." And needless to say they found out and fired both of us. The superintendent called me in and said, "You little ungrateful black bastard." That ended that job for the both of us.

My father never complained. He said we'll find a job somewhere else, so we left there and headed for Michigan. We got a bus and headed here, and he got a job at a place called Burns, Gibson and Raymond, 6400 Miller, off of Mt. Elliott. He worked over there for about a month and you guessed it, he had a job for me over there, as well. He got elected as steward on second shift. When the union members found out, they went on strike, and threatened to shut the company down. He was really disappointed in the union, but was deter-

104

mined not to allow them to control his life, so to speak. They asked him to resign just because he was Black. He told them he would think about it. He asked a guy that worked with him from Kentucky, a guy named James Nichols, a hillbilly from the hills of Kentucky. He couldn't read or write, but my father felt he was a good person. My father asked him to assume the role of steward, and he said, "Well, I can't read or write," and my father said, "Well, I'll train you." And he did. He'd bring him home with him, and they would sit down and he'd learn how to read and write. He learned to read the contracts, and do a lot of different things. When he said he was ready, my father said, "I'm going to resign now, and when I resign they'll post the job and we're going to get you elected." And that's exactly what happened.

I ran into racism again when I tried to volunteer into the Navy. I was told they didn't accept Blacks. So I got a job at Detroit Double Gear, which at that point, was next to Dodge Main. In 1945, Truman began to straighten out the business with the Navy. I volunteered then and they accepted me. It was the first integrated Navy company that went through Great Lakes. By the time I got out of the service and was hired at GM, I'd been active in the union, civil rights movement, and politics. I was still in love with A. Philip Randolph, getting mail, and reading three or four papers a day. There was the Michigan Chronicle, the Detroit News, Detroit Free Press, Detroit Times.

The late Nelson Jack Edwards was one of the greatest human beings I've ever met, one of the outstanding world trade unionists. Only if we take a serious look at world history will we dig up the significance of the things he did. He had a profound impact on the work of Martin Luther King and the labor movement. He was one of the giants of the labor movement. His life was snuffed out in a bar he owned right here in the city of Detroit, and it's one of those kinds of things that you can't replace.

Today the union is significantly stronger, more effective, with more resources and a deeper social conscious than there's ever been since the inception of the labor. I'd say that in the broad sense, that it transcends nationalism. Labor is the last group to gain power in the body of politics and it's not limited to national or nations.

I suggest two pamphlets: one entitled "The Future of Work", and the other one is something put out by the AFL-CIO Committee on the evolution of work, called "The Changing of Situations of Workers and Their Unions." Both are small reports, yet two of the best reports that I've encountered in the last 25 or 30 years. They represent 20 years of research, pulled together by some imminent people. They give a critical analysis of the strength and weakness of the trade unions. The point is Poland just elected a trade union, and in Japan, trade unions are playing a significant role in its structure. The trade union is the last frontier to become a world power.